# Praise for *Using Generative AI for SEO*

A lifeline for digital marketers! This book is not some kind of simplistic swipe file—it is a treasure map from experienced pros that allows you to gracefully thrive in the AI era. Highly recommended, and guaranteed to supercharge your SEO skills!

*—Tim Ash, CEO, SiteTuners; author of* Landing Page Optimization

Being a successful SEO isn't for the faint of heart or the impatient. Continuous learning is essential for growth, but learning takes time—and time is money. Luckily, Eric and Adrián's new book is your one-stop, in-depth reference for leveraging generative AI to boost your SEO efforts. It explains how strategically combining the power of generative AI and core SEO principles will improve content quality and achieve better organic visibility. This is one book you'll want to make time for; it will be time well spent.

*—Debra Mastaler, Founder, Alliance-Link and De9eR Media; Columnist,* Search Engine Land; *speaker and trainer*

Eric and Adrián have compiled a foundational book for stepping into the new and confusing world of generative AI optimization. Clearly written, fact-based, and full of supporting information for further followup, this book will help you understand where we are today and where we're heading tomorrow!

*—Duane Forrester, COO, LynxPulse; former Senior Vice President of Search, INDEXR.ai; author of* How to Make Money with Your Blog *and* Turn Clicks into Customers

Eric Enge literally wrote the book on SEO with his *Art of SEO*. Now he has done it again, partnering with Adrián Ridner and writing the book on this new age of generative AI and SEO. It's all here—everything you need to know about AI search. Eric is a born teacher, so this book is the place to go to school.

—*Mark Traphagen, Vice President of Product Marketing and Training, seoClarity; speaker and writer*

Eric has been at the forefront of SEO for decades and remains so. He and Adrián have done a stellar job laying out practical (read: actually useful) ways to apply AI to accelerate your SEO. This book is a must-have for any modern SEO.

—*Zac Carman, CEO, ConsumerAffairs.com; Entrepreneur in Residence, Mainsail Partners*

Eric's years of experience, expertise, and passion are evident in his latest work. In an age of overreaction to AI, it is a breath of fresh air to read a deeply thought-out, measured approach to how AI can enhance your SEO strategy. This book is full of practical advice you can use immediately.

—*Todd Friesen, former VP of Digital Experience and SEO, Vimeo; former Director of SEO and Digital Strategy, Salesforce*

Although *Using Generative AI for SEO* is geared toward anyone interested in SEO, AI, GEO, and search in general, it really sets the 99% apart from the 1%. From new AI engines, to embedded vectors that brought in phrase relational space, to GEO, this text will lift everyone like no other search industry–related book. It is truly an in-depth book about a craft that is part science, art, technology, psychology, and ultimately...marketing!!!

—*Sean Kainec, Partner and Head Digital Strategist, Quattro Agency*

I've known Eric Enge for over 20 years now, and there are few who have his depth of knowledge, understanding, and historical perspective of how search works and how search will change. He has spoken directly with countless search engineers and has tested countless algorithmic theories over the years. Eric is a visionary and a go-to resource when it comes to SEO, search, and how AI is changing this landscape.

—*Barry Schwartz, President, RustyBrick; Editor,* Search Engine Roundtable; *News Editor,* Search Engine Land

If you're looking for facts, not fluff, on how to successfully build SEO campaigns in an AI world, you should read *Using Generative AI for SEO.* Both Eric Enge and Adrián Ridner bring a wealth of experience in working with real-world companies and employ solid, data-backed strategies for growing visibility in the age of AI. Highly recommended.

—*Cyrus Sheppard, Founder, Zyppy SEO; former Chief SEO Strategist, Moz*

With 20+ years of SEO experience, the level of detail in and the how-to nature of Eric's *Using Generative AI for SEO* come as no surprise. The delight is how accessible his ideas are to the uninitiated. This book is, at turns, educational, technical, sociological, philosophical, inspirational, and operational. Keep this tome handy as a way to understand our new world, as a reference book for quick concept refreshers, and as a handbook for your to-do list.

—*Jim Sterne, Founder, Santa Barbara AI Collective; President, Target Marketing of Santa Barbara; author, speaker, and trainer*

We are in the midst of a generational shift in how people will discover information on the internet, and this book is required reading for anyone who seeks for their online marketing to remain relevant in this changing world. Eric is an absolute sage at SEO, and there's no better author to help both newbies and experienced marketers weather these turbulent times.

—*Eli Schwartz, Growth Advisor; author of* Product-Led SEO

With all the hype surrounding AI these days, it's refreshing to see a book that shows how AI complements rather than replaces skilled SEO. In this rapidly shifting environment, where every tool and technique applied smartly can make the difference between visibility and obscurity, Eric and Adrián's words of wisdom should be heeded by all intelligent search marketers.

—*Chris Sherman, former Founding Editor of* Search Engine Land

# Using Generative AI
# for SEO

*AI-First Strategies to Improve*
*Quality, Efficiency, and Costs*

Eric Enge and Adrián Ridner

**Using Generative AI for SEO**

by Eric Enge and Adrián Ridner

Published by O'Reilly Media, Inc., 1005 Gravenstein Highway North, Sebastopol, CA 95472.

O'Reilly books may be purchased for educational, business, or sales promotional use. Online editions are also available for most titles (*http://oreilly.com*). For more information, contact our corporate/institutional sales department: 800-998-9938 or *corporate@oreilly.com*.

**Acquisitions Editor:** David Michelson

**Development Editors:** Virginia Wilson and Rita Fernando

**Production Editor:** Gregory Hyman

**Copyeditor:** Shannon Turlington

**Proofreader:** Stephanie English

**Indexer:** nSight, Inc.

**Cover Designer:** Susan Thompson

**Cover Illustrator:** Susan Thompson

**Interior Designer:** Monica Kamsvaag

**Interior Illustrator:** Kate Dullea

July 2025:     First Edition

**Revision History for the First Edition**

2025-07-02:   First Release

See *http://oreilly.com/catalog/errata.csp?isbn=9781098167202* for release details.

978-1-098-16720-2

[LSI]

# Contents

# Preface

OpenAI's launch of ChatGPT in November 2022 marked the start of a new technology revolution. This has driven a rapid demand for generative AI applications within organizations across the globe. With that explosion of demand came a whole host of ways to use generative AI that intersect with search engine optimization (SEO).

In addition, major players, such as Google, Microsoft, Apple, Meta, and Amazon, have all leapt into the AI space and are making huge investments in applying AI technology. Newcomers such as Anthropic and Perplexity have also made their mark.

The purpose of this book is to provide a comprehensive education on what this technology is and how you can use it to drive your SEO program. Included are discussions of how you can use generative AI in your program today and how it will evolve and change in the future. Overall, our goal is to help you decide how you want to use generative AI and get your program into full gear.

## Who Should Read This Book

If you're interested in learning about AI and SEO, you should read this book. It will expose you to all aspects of how generative AI can enhance your SEO program and will have laid the necessary groundwork for becoming a more effective digital marketer and a more educated SEO professional.

An experienced SEO practitioner will find this volume invaluable as an extensive reference to use generative AI in ongoing SEO engagements: both internally, within an in-house SEO group or SEO consultancy, and externally, with SEO clients.

In short, anyone with a background or interest in SEO, ranging from newcomers to advanced SEOs, to executives who manage organizations that execute SEO programs. The economic advantages of using a properly applied AI program to enhance your SEO strategy are significant and shouldn't be overlooked. So climb on board, strap on your seatbelt, and get ready for an incredible ride!

## What You Will Learn

Our goal with this book is to provide you with a solid foundation that will enable you to get started leveraging generative AI to help drive SEO in your organization.

In Part I, "AI and SEO Essentials", you'll learn about SEO in the age of generative AI and some background on generative AI. In Part II, "Putting AI to Work", you'll learn how to start leveraging generative AI in your organization and how to use it to scale your content development and technical SEO efforts. Finally, in Part III, "The Next Level of AI-Driven SEO", you'll learn about advanced use cases for generative AI and SEO, and AI risks and challenges you should be aware of, and we'll also take a look into the future of generative AI and SEO.

## Conventions Used in This Book

The following typographical conventions are used in this book:

*Italic*
> Indicates new terms, URLs, email addresses, and filenames.

`Constant width`
> Used for program listings, as well as within paragraphs to refer to program elements such as variable or function names, databases, data types, environment variables, statements, and keywords.

## O'Reilly Online Learning

 For more than 40 years, *O'Reilly Media* has provided technology and business training, knowledge, and insight to help companies succeed.

Our unique network of experts and innovators share their knowledge and expertise through books, articles, and our online learning platform. O'Reilly's online learning platform gives you on-demand access to live training courses, in-depth learning paths, interactive coding environments, and a vast collection of text and video from O'Reilly and 200+ other publishers. For more information, visit *https://oreilly.com*.

## How to Contact Us

Please address comments and questions concerning this book to the publisher:

O'Reilly Media, Inc.

1005 Gravenstein Highway North

Sebastopol, CA 95472

800-889-8969 (in the United States or Canada)

707-827-7019 (international or local)

707-829-0104 (fax)

*support@oreilly.com*

*https://oreilly.com/about/contact.html*

We have a web page for this book, where we list errata, examples, and any additional information. You can access this page at *https://oreil.ly/genai-for-seo*.

For news and information about our books and courses, visit *https://oreilly.com*.

Find us on LinkedIn: *https://linkedin.com/company/oreilly-media*

Watch us on YouTube: *https://youtube.com/oreillymedia*

# PART I

# AI and SEO Essentials

# SEO in the Age of Generative AI

The age of artificial intelligence is upon us. AI will have broad, sweeping implications that will affect nearly every aspect of our lives, including how users search for what they need online. Therefore, we must adapt how we perform search engine optimization (SEO) to get our brands in front of users. In this book, we'll look beyond the hype and myths, instead focusing on the generative AI tools that exist today and how they can be used to substantially enhance your SEO program.

In this chapter, we'll discuss why organic search remains one of the most valuable marketing channels at your disposal, why SEO is the key to optimizing the volume of traffic you get from that channel, and why generative AI tools won't cause that to change. You'll learn how the Google algorithm really works by taking a deep dive into Google's 2023 testimony to the United States Department of Justice (DOJ) (*https://oreil.ly/ozo-N*) and the Google Content Warehouse API leak (*https://oreil.ly/oGoa8*), which became widely known in May 2024.

You'll notice that some of what we say in this chapter will differ from commonly held beliefs about how SEO works. Keep an open mind. This information will come in handy if you're responsible for obtaining resources or budgets to execute SEO programs. It may help you educate and gain support from those who hold fast to outdated beliefs. Having a sound understanding of core parts of the Google algorithm will also better equip you to use generative AI as a tool to enhance your SEO efforts.

Here is what we'll cover in this chapter:

- Key terms
- Why SEO matters

- The Google algorithm
- What you need to know about what Google wants
- Common technical SEO problems you need to know about
- What you need to know about content SEO

Each of these sections will take into account the impact of generative AI plus what we learned from Google's testimony to the US DOJ and the Google API leak.

## Key Terms

We will use the following key terms frequently throughout this book:

*Search engine optimization (SEO)*
> The practice of making changes to your website (such as technical changes, content additions, interlinking, etc.) with the goal of earning more traffic from search engine referrals. SEO generally involves building a website that provides great value to users and ensuring that search engines can easily read and understand the site (i.e., that it is "search engine friendly").

*Technical SEO*
> A subset of SEO that focuses on technical changes to your website. These changes can take many forms, such as implementing a new ecommerce platform, changing JavaScript frameworks, implementing SEO tags (e.g., `rel=canonical`, `noindex`, `nofollow`, and `hreflang`), and ensuring that your website is easily crawled. The main purpose of technical SEO is to ensure that search engine robots can crawl and understand the content of your web pages.

*Content SEO*
> A subset of SEO involving the creation of high-value content that search engines can consider for ranking in their search results. This includes understanding what content would be most helpful to users, creating it, and publishing it on your website.

*EEAT (experience, expertise, authoritativeness, and trustworthiness)*
> Refers to a variety of factors that Google suggests are related to adding value for users and how well your organization and website are received in the market. Many in the industry think of this as a direct ranking factor, but for most sites, other than health and financial sites, it's not. However,

Google does track other factors that having good EEAT should affect. We'll discuss this more in Chapter 3.

*Click-through rate (CTR)*
A calculation of the percentage of users who click on a link, such as a link in the search results. For example, if one hundred people view a search result and four people click a link in the results, we say that the CTR for that link is 4%.

*Conversion rate*
A calculation of the percentage of visitors to a web page who convert into a lead, sign-up, or sale (aka "conversions"). For example, if one hundred people visit a web page and five of them convert, the conversion rate would be 5%.

*Generative AI*
A type of artificial intelligence that is trained on large amounts of data, such as text, images, and video, and then can respond to user prompts with text, image, or video responses. Generative AI tools include ChatGPT, Microsoft Copilot, Gemini, and Claude.

Now that we have a common language, let's talk about SEO and its role in the success of your organization.

## Why Does SEO Matter?

There are several key reasons why SEO can be so valuable to your organization:

- Organic search is one of the largest sources of traffic to most websites.
- SEO offers one of the highest conversion rates among digital marketing channels.
- The return on investment (ROI) potential of SEO is one of the highest among digital marketing channels.

Let's explore these three reasons in detail.

### HIGH TRAFFIC POTENTIAL

Organic search remains one of the highest sources of traffic to most of the world's websites. But why is the potential for traffic so high? Simply because there are so many searches on Google: 8.5 billion per day (*https://oreil.ly/Z3LYm*), or 99,000 queries per second. In addition, 53% of all clicks come from organic search, according to research (*https://oreil.ly/gW073*) performed by BrightEdge Research in 2020 (see Figure 1-1). More recently, studies (*https://oreil.ly/imesf*) have suggested that the advent of AI Overviews has lowered SEO traffic potential by 35%, but even with this reduction SEO remains a highly valuable channel. Therefore, SEO to put yourself ahead of your competitors on the search results page is of critical importance to your organization.

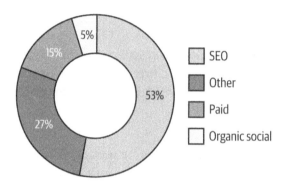

*Figure 1-1. The highest percentage of clicks (53%) are from organic search (data source: Bright-edge Research, "Organic Channel Share Expands to 53.3% of Traffic," 2019 (https://oreil.ly/gW073))*

You can also see in Figure 1-1 that SEO provides 10 times more traffic than organic social media. Note that this percentage is calculated over the lifetime of the content; for organizations with a strong social media presence, social media may provide a larger share of traffic at the time of the content's initial publication.

There has been a lot of speculation that generative AI tools will dramatically reduce the demand for traditional search engines, but this is extremely unlikely. In fact, data published by Rand Fishkin of SparkToro in March 2025 (*https://oreil.ly/GeEoZ*) shows that Google still has a 93.57% market share. Generative AI will have some impact, but its propensity to make errors will hold it back from replacing search. In addition, there are classes of queries that aren't great fits for generative AI, such as when a user isn't likely to be satisfied by a mostly accurate, mostly complete text response. A few examples include:

- A user has a medical condition, so they are going to do extensive research and will want answers they know are both 100% accurate and complete.
- A user needs to obtain comprehensive knowledge of a topic, so they are going to want to perform detailed research. Examples of this include

understanding the steps in building a bridge or learning Python well enough to execute complex programming tasks.

- A user wants assistance in preparing for a career certification test (such as the Praxis teacher's exam).

- A user has an immediate real-time need, such as locating a nearby business (e.g., local search queries like "pizza near me").

Gartner (*https://oreil.ly/PR6xo*) forecast a reduction of search engine demand of 25% by 2026. This would be a material—but not dramatic—reduction. Search demand will remain highly relevant to your organization.

## HIGH CONVERSION RATES

Another reason that organic search traffic is so valuable is that it has a high conversion rate. Data from Sage Consulting (*https://oreil.ly/6q7Tg*), as shown in Figure 1-2, demonstrates the conversion rate across many different channels, and SEO is among the best.

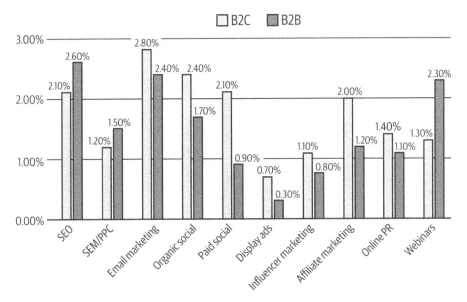

*Figure 1-2. Digital marketing conversion rates (data source: Sage Consulting, "Digital Marketing Conversion Rates: 2025 Report," 2025 (https://oreil.ly/6q7Tg))*

SEO conversion rates tend to be high because users who enter a search query have a purpose. They want something, be that to get information, complete a task, or research or buy a product or service. When they click on a search result, that implies they believe the result fits their needs.

Once the user enters your site, you have a motivated customer, which will potentially result in a desired action for your organization, such as a purchase, a sign-up for a newsletter, and so on. Even if all they want is information, they will still associate some value with your organization and website if you're the one to provide them with what they're looking for.

## HIGH ROI

The high conversion rate of SEO is a large factor in why SEO can lead to very high ROI. SEO ROI can be difficult to measure due to the delay in the time from when you implement technical or content SEO and when you see the benefits. This often takes three to six months. Note that conversion rates will vary significantly depending on the products or services offered by the site.

For that reason, there is little data on SEO ROI. Some agencies have published their own assessments of ROI, though. For example, Terakeet (*https://oreil.ly/qo6Vg*) reports that SEO ROI ranges between 5x and 12.2x, and Profitworks (*https://oreil.ly/AnWat*) reported an SEO ROI of 2.75x. Figure 1-3 shows the results of a *Search Engine Journal* survey of digital marketers (*https://oreil.ly/11aJ9*) finding that 49% consider SEO to be the highest ROI channel.

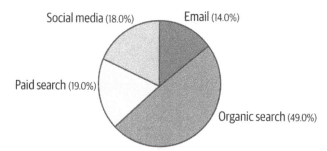

*Figure 1-3. Highest ROI channels (data source: Search Engine Journal, "Which Digital Marketing Channel Has the Highest ROI for Your Website?" 2018 (https://oreil.ly/6q7Tg))*

Another reason that SEO ROI is high is there is no cost per action, or "sales cost." For example, with pay-per-click (PPC) models, you pay for each click on your ad. Similarly, with display advertising, you pay for your ad placement (per impression, per click, or per action). As a result, there is a direct cost associated with each sale you make from your advertising, which you pay to third parties for your ad placements. That said, the advantage of these models is that they are "direct response" models, meaning that for every dollar you spend you can expect to receive some money back in the short term. The predictability of these models is high, and they can usually be tuned to drive revenue at a known level of ROI. The downside with direct response models, though, is that the competition for ad placements is very high because of how direct and immediate the response is, which drives prices up and causes ROI to be comparatively low.

SEO isn't a direct response model. When you invest in SEO, it may take three to six months to see results, and the scale of the results is difficult to forecast. In addition, no money is paid to third parties: with SEO, your content that ranks high in Google search results has earned that placement, and you did not have to pay Google for your presence there.

There is a cost to SEO, of course, which is the amount of money you invest in the team you have that works on SEO on your behalf as well as others who collaborate with the SEO team (such as development and writing teams). But because there is less certainty of the rankings and traffic you might get as a result of your investment in SEO, many senior managers are reluctant to make the investment, or they limit the size of that investment. This frequently leads to their not taking advantage of many opportunities to grow their organic search traffic. (Note: if you use generative AI to assist in your SEO efforts, the cost of those efforts will be less and will lower the risk associated with the investment. Hence the reason for this book!) This opens the door for more aggressive organizations to make those investments and take advantage of those opportunities. As a result, they can gain access to higher ROI conversions.

As you can see, optimizing your organization's websites so that they appear when potential customers have the most incentive to visit them can be exceptionally valuable. As such, it pays to understand how search engine algorithms work so that you can optimize your SEO strategy.

## The Google Algorithm

In May 2024, an anonymous source made Rand Fishkin aware of documents leaked from Google (*https://oreil.ly/oGoa8*) that provided detailed information on more than 2,500 pages of API information, including names of modules and more than 10,000 parameters that Google uses in its algorithms. This extraordinary information helped clarify how Google is able to measure many aspects of websites, including the quality of the content on those sites.

What has attracted less attention from SEO professionals is the wealth of information related to how the Google algorithm works in Google's testimony to the US DOJ in 2023. Of particular interest was an internal presentation (*https://oreil.ly/G1E43*) given by Google to the DOJ. This slide deck specifically outlines aspects of how the Google algorithm works. Figures 1-4 through 1-8 are slides from that presentation, which was released to the public by the US DOJ. You should review these slides in detail as they illustrate key concepts of Google's algorithm that are important to your SEO optimization efforts.

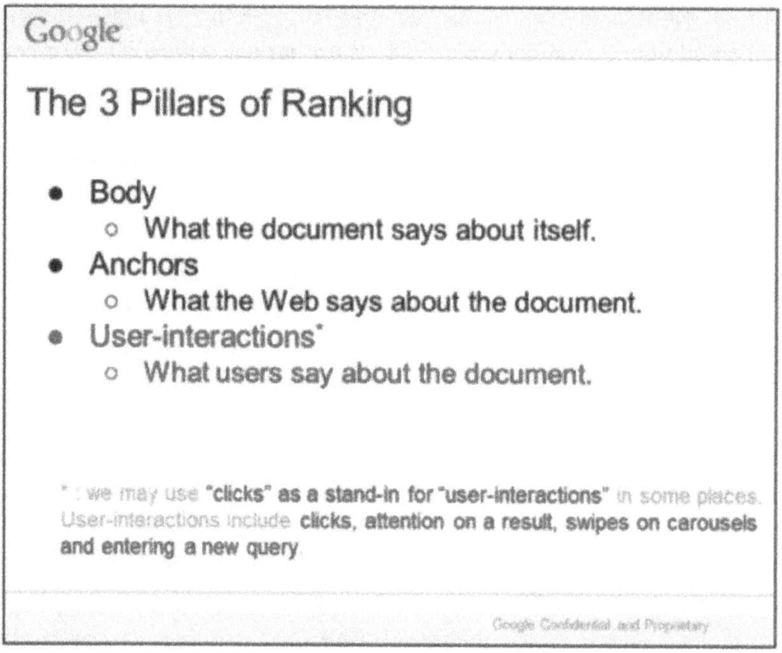

*Figure 1-4. Google internal presentation: the three pillars of ranking (source: US Department of Justice (https://oreil.ly/G1E43))*

As you can see in Figure 1-4, Google indicates that ranking is broken into three broad concepts:

- "What the document says about itself" relates to the nature of the content itself. This is where the words and phrases used in a piece of content establish its relevance. Title tags, heading tags, bolding, italics, and font size all play a role in highlighting the parts of the content that are the most important.

- "What the Web says about the document" refers to the role of links in ranking, so these are still an important ranking factor.

- "What users say about the document" is a measure of user engagement with the document, where higher levels of engagement imply that the document is of higher quality.

Also take note of the text at the bottom of the slide. Here the presentation indicates that user interactions tracked include clicks, attention on a result, swipes on carousels, and entering a new query.

The "user interaction signals" slide, shown in Figure 1-5, clearly establishes the concept that data on user interactions on a page that receives traffic from a Google search is fed back to Google and this can influence future search results. The interactions specified on this slide include read, clicks, scrolls, and mouse hovers. Between Figures 1-4 and 1-5 you can see that Google is interested in many aspects of user interactions.

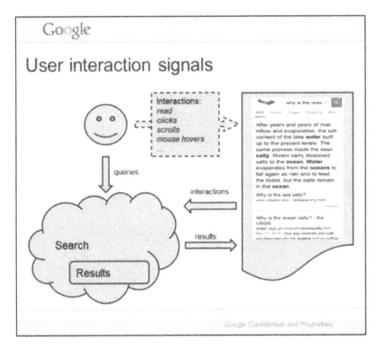

*Figure 1-5. Google internal presentation: user interaction signals (source: US Department of Justice (https://oreil.ly/G1E43))*

The slide shown in Figure 1-6 is arguably one of the most interesting slides of them all because of its title: "We do not understand documents. We fake it." Then Google clarifies that it watches how people react to documents and collects and stores data on that. What this makes clear to us is that Google places a great deal of weight on these user-interaction signals.

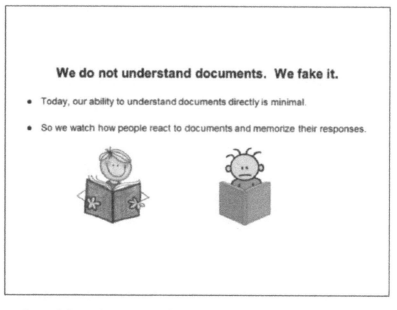

Figure 1-6. Google internal presentation: how Google understands documents (source: US Department of Justice (https://oreil.ly/G1E43))

The slide shown in Figure 1-7 helps clarify that this data is fed back into the system and used to benefit future users.

Finally, the slide shown in Figure 1-8 closes the loop and establishes that the user-interaction data is used to improve search results, which is how it benefits future users. You can see more slides from this deck in an excellent article from Search Engine Land by Danny Goodwin: "Seven Must-See Google Search Ranking Documents in Antitrust Trial Exhibits" (https://oreil.ly/dqOM9).

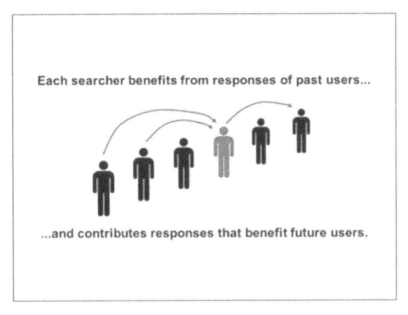

*Figure 1-7. Google internal presentation: user interactions are stored by Google (source: US Department of Justice (https://oreil.ly/G1E43))*

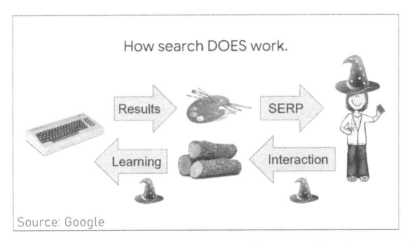

*Figure 1-8. Google internal presentation: user interactions improve search results (source: US Department of Justice (https://oreil.ly/G1E43))*

Google VP of Search Pandurang Nayak also testified to the DOJ (*https://oreil.ly/lyYES*) about how the Google algorithm works. In this testimony, he made many fascinating observations, including these two:

- Google has been tracking user-interaction data since 2005, possibly even earlier, and using that data as a key part of its ranking algorithms.

- Google's primary goal in launching the Chrome browser in 2008 was to collect even more user-interaction data.

Last but not least, we have the information contained within the Google API leak documents (*https://oreil.ly/fixv1*). Parsing through these documents is not for the faint of heart because there are more than 2,400 of them. In short, what these documents allow us to see is that Google has large numbers of parameters related to user interaction. This includes more than 30 variables related to clicks as well as variables related to hovers, scrolls, and a lot more.

In summary, Google leverages interactions with its search results and data from Chrome to help understand which web pages best address which search queries and which content is the highest quality. This includes studying click patterns and other aspects of the behavior of users on your website. For this reason, creating a great user experience (UX) on your website is an important part of SEO.

## What You Need to Know About What Google Wants

In this section, we'll discuss what type of content the Google algorithm is designed to find and rank. Our discussion will include the highly valuable information that we learned from the Google API leak. We'll discuss that from the perspective of what you need to do to get your content to rank higher in Google Search.

Earning organic search traffic happens after you have accomplished these three things:

- Ensured that search engines (primarily Google in the great majority of countries) can read and process your website. This is accomplished by a well-thought-out approach to the technology used in building your site.

- Published great content that does an excellent job of helping users on your website. One of the principal ways that Google measures the quality of your web pages and website is by measuring user interactions that take place on the site to see if users are having a good experience.

- Earned a level of reputation and visibility in the market that suggests that your content is in demand (causing Google to want to rank it). Google evaluates links to your site from other websites to measure this. In addition, traffic from other sources, including social media sites, emails, browser bookmarks, and type-in traffic, are all indications that your site has a strong reputation.

### Note

The more relevant and valuable the links are to the visitors of the web page containing the link, the better. If users are clicking on the links and coming to your site, the links have much more SEO value to you.

There are also sites that can detract from your brand. If you publish on third-party sites that have a lot of low-quality content, that won't reflect well on your brand. This is data that Google can track using Chrome.

For decades, many SEO professionals focused on finding ways to manipulate Google's rankings to their advantage. While most SEO professionals tried to play by the rules, those who didn't created enough problems that Google has had to invest significant resources to uncover their tactics. In response, Google has created many algorithms intended to fight spam in the search results. Google also maintains a large team of "web spam" professionals who can evaluate potential problem sites and assign manual ranking penalties.

The reason this matters to Google is because the success of its search engine ultimately depends on its ability to deliver the best possible results to users. User satisfaction with the search results drives higher levels of usage and helps Google preserve its market share. This has resulted in extremely high satisfaction rates with Google. In 2024, this figure was at 81% according to a survey in *Search Engine Land* (*https://oreil.ly/1Z1vd*).

Google accomplishes this with the quality of its search results. This depends on many factors, but the goals of all of Google's efforts are as follows:

- Understand the user's intent with a query
- Discover great content on all topics across the web
- Match up great content relevant to a user's query and deliver that to the user in the search results

This leads to the core of what Google wants from websites: high-quality content combined with a great UX. We can see confirmation of that in Figure 1-9 showing tweets from Google spokespeople since 2018.

Figure 1-9. *Google wants great content*

## HIGH-QUALITY CONTENT IS CRITICAL TO SEO SUCCESS

What this all means is that the best strategies for your SEO program center on creating great content designed to help users with their wants and needs. As you delve into how to use AI to grow your SEO program later in this book, you will learn how AI can assist with creating that great content.

The following are some key ways you can influence the quality of your content:

- The subject matter expertise of the author and the level of scrutiny in the review and feedback process

- The author's level of direct experience with the content

- Whether the content brings unique new expertise or perspectives on the topic

Doing this well requires a deep commitment to understanding user needs related to your business and finding ways to meet those needs better than the websites that compete with yours. Google has a page (*https://oreil.ly/laoAh*)

dedicated to outlining how it suggests content creators meet these goals. Google also considers two other factors:

- Whether your site is considered authoritative on the topic
- If users trust your organization and website in your chosen subject area

### Note

Analysis performed by the authors of the algorithms used by generative AI tool providers shows that they likewise have an interest in very high quality content. As a result, any investment you make in such content will potentially assist you with ranking in SEO, ChatGPT Search, and other LLM-based search tools.

### PROVIDE SITE VISITORS WITH A GREAT USER EXPERIENCE

As you saw in the "The Google Algorithm" on page 9, Google directly measures user interactions on the pages of your site to learn about the quality of your content. It's also likely that Google looks at this in an aggregated form to understand the strength of your brand. Based on this alone, it's already clear that you need to treat UX as an important SEO ranking factor.

We saw in Figure 1-9 that Google regularly tells webmasters that they need to publish high-quality content. Google has communicated this need to create a high-quality UX in a variety of ways, including:

- EEAT
- Core web vitals
- Interstitial penalties
- Need for secure websites (HTTPS)
- Detection and flagging of hacked websites

We'll explore these next.

### EEAT

We introduced the concept of experience, expertise, authoritativeness, and trust in the beginning of this chapter. These are guidelines that Google has offered to website publishers to help them evaluate the likelihood that they are creating content of value to users. Google can't measure EEAT directly but looks at a variety of other signals to measure the quality of your content. This includes directly measuring the behavior of users on your site to determine if they seem to be finding what they were looking for based on factors such as how long they spend on your site, whether they return to your site, how many appear to have a good versus a bad experience, and more.

Per the API leak, Google appears to also track authors of documents, so there may be some signal related to the typical engagement that content from that author gets. In March 2025, Google's John Mueller confirmed that Google does track these types of signals for what Google calls "Your Money or Your Life (YMYL)" pages: pages related to health or finances. However, he also said that they don't keep track of this information for sites that aren't focused on YMYL topics. In addition, a detailed examination of the documents (*https://oreil.ly/fixv1*) contained in the 2024 Google API leak provides no evidence that Google actually tracks "experience," "expertise," "authoritativeness," and "trustworthiness" other than the author. Based on this, it seems likely that most of what goes into evaluating content quality is based on actual user engagement with the content.

## Core web vitals

In 2020, Google introduced the concept of *core web vitals*: a set of signals related to the performance of rendering a web page. These initially included:

*Largest contentful paint (LCP)*
> Measures how long it takes to see a substantial portion of the content requested

*First input delay (FID)*
> Measures responsiveness to user input

*Cumulative layout shift (CLS)*
> Measures how stable the web page is while it's rendering

In 2024, Google replaced FID with interaction to next paint (INP), which also measures responsiveness of the user interface. Google made the switch to INP because it believes that INP provides a better measure of the page load time's impact on the quality of the UX on the page.

Data from the Google API leak shows that Google actively tracks these signals within its ranking systems. However, it is not known how much weight is placed on these signals. In addition, if your web pages are materially slower than that of your competitors, you might see lower user engagement signals than your competitors do, and this is likely to be the most important reason for you to ensure that your pages load quickly.

## Interstitial penalties, HTTPS, and hacked websites

Google (*https://oreil.ly/uTgL7*) has announced three other signals that are related to the UX on a website:

*Interstitial penalties*
> If Google detects an interstitial that loads on initial page load on top of the content that the user is looking for, that can provide a negative ranking boost on that page.

*Secure websites (HTTPS)*
> In 2014, Google made a big push to get website publishers to implement HTTPS encryption on their websites. While this is a standard today, it wasn't at the time. Using HTTPS provides greater assurance that the user will get the actual content they requested, as opposed to something that has been altered during the process of traveling from your web server to their browser (for more on this, search "man-in-the-middle attacks").

*Hacked websites*
> Google will also flag web sites that have been hacked. These sites can be blocked in Google Search and Chrome. The main reason for doing this is to protect users from bad experiences.

These UX signals are in addition to what we discussed in "The Google Algorithm" on page 9. It should be clear that user engagement is a large ranking factor—possibly the second largest ranking signal, trailing only the relevance of the content to the user's query.

### GOOGLE'S ALGORITHM HAS LIMITATIONS

There are some limitations to Google's ability to process a web page. Issues that you need to be aware of include the following:

- JavaScript implementations can affect crawlability.
- Limitations of ecommerce and content management systems (CMS) can also block effective crawling.
- Google wants us to use schema markup to help it better understand site content.

- Google wants us to use hreflang tags so that it's easier to be clear what languages or countries various pages of your site are targeting.

- Google wants us to use link attributes, such as nofollow, sponsored, and UGC (user-generated content), to help it identify links that are not meant as true endorsements or citations.

- You need to create a great UX for your site (including page speed).

- When you move content, you need to implement 301 redirects.

These are just some examples of issues that you may need to address so that Google can find and understand all the valuable content on your websites.

---

### Key Resource: The Art of SEO

This chapter provides only a basic introduction to SEO. If you want to dive into that topic more completely, we recommend starting with *The Art of SEO: Mastering Search Engine Optimization* by Eric Enge, Stephan Spencer, and Jessie Stricchiola (O'Reilly), which provides a complete guide to all aspects of SEO. This book is now in its fourth edition.

---

## Common Technical SEO Problems You Need to Know About

In the last section, we raised some of the key limitations of Google Search. These are all examples of issues that need to be fixed by making changes to your website, other than simply publishing new content. We call these *technical SEO issues*: things you need to address to help Google understand your website. We'll discuss some of these next.

### JAVASCRIPT, ECOMMERCE PLATFORMS, AND CMS

Each development environment brings a great deal of value to website development. They make websites far easier to build, modify, and support. However, each of these systems comes with limitations. While they provide structures that simplify the development process, those structures can potentially cause problems. Let's look at each of these in a bit more detail:

*JavaScript frameworks and static site generators (SSGs)*

As of 2025, 98.8% of websites use some level of JavaScript (*https://oreil.ly/ 4NDGd*), which often comes in the form of JavaScript frameworks or SSGs. They can make it difficult to crawl the site, cause the site to be very slow, make it harder to implement custom title tags, and more. Properly addressing these concerns requires that you perform detailed research on the limitations of whichever platform you choose and then have your dev team make the changes required to address the limitations.

*Ecommerce platforms and CMS*

About 67% of all websites use a CMS, and more than 25% of the top one million websites use an ecommerce platform (*https://oreil.ly/bnOjU*). Figure 1-10 shows the most popular ecommerce platforms by market share as of April 3, 2025, according to BuiltWith. Just as with JavaScript, these platforms all come with their own limitations. Even a simple CMS like WordPress requires that you use a plug-in to help set it up for SEO. Popular plug-ins like the Yoast SEO plug-in make it easy to edit post title tags and meta descriptions and to add SEO tags. Without such plug-ins, these things can't be done. On the ecommerce platform, issues also need to be addressed. For example, Shopify requires a plug-in to optimize for SEO (*https://oreil.ly/QPrN9*), and Magento optimization requires that you install plug-ins such as Amasty or Mageworx.

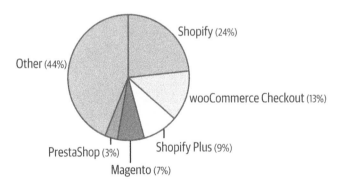

*Figure 1-10. Most popular ecommerce platforms by market share (data source: BuiltWith, "Ecommerce Usage Distribution in the Top One Million Sites," 2025 (https://oreil.ly/fruos))*

## OTHER TECHNICAL SEO AREAS TO ADDRESS

In addition to issues with development environments, there are many ways Google has asked website owners to provide more information about their sites:

*Structured data*

> Google suggests that site owners implement structured data to help it better understand the content. Schema.org (*https://schema.org/*), an initiative introduced by Google, Bing, and Yahoo! in 2011, is the standard for structured data. In return for implementing this schema on your site, search engines can show your page in the search results with enhanced formatting. Figure 1-11 shows an example of an enhanced search result that is the result of implementing schema.

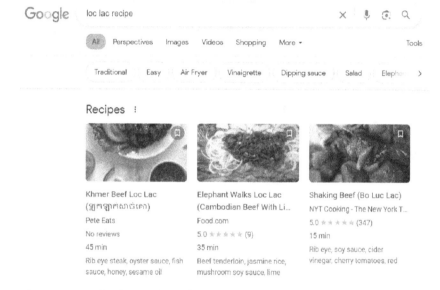

*Figure 1-11. Sample schema-enhanced search results*

*Hreflang*

> If you have websites that support multiple languages, Google wants you to implement hreflang tags. These tags help Google (and Bing) see that the different versions of your pages are not duplicate content because they are targeted at different countries. Figure 1-12 shows a simplified example of what an hreflang implementation looks like.

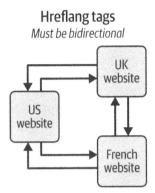

*Figure 1-12. Hreflang tag implementation*

*.htaccess files*

These files have many different uses. Two of the most popular ones that relate to SEO are 301 redirecting URLs and blocking bots from accessing some web pages or portions of your site. For example, you may want to block malicious crawlers from accessing any of the pages of your site, or you may have content that you moved from one URL to another.

*Robots.txt*

Webmasters also use *robots.txt* to guide how their sites are crawled. Typically, you should use *robots.txt* to limit the behavior of legitimate crawlers, such as search engines, and *.htaccess* to block crawling by malicious crawlers.

*Core web vitals*

These relate to the performance of your site. Google looks at three major metrics: LCP measures how quickly the main content of your page loads; INP measures how quickly your web servers are able to visibly respond to user requests; and CLS measures how much the layout of your page jumps around during rendering of the page.

*Development team issues*

The developers within your organization generally try to do the right thing whenever they're working on a project on your website. But like anyone else, they are under pressure to meet deadlines, and they probably don't know SEO that well, if at all. This means mistakes can often happen during development. You need to have the right processes in place to ensure that each of your website updates are reviewed for SEO before they are launched.

AI can help to varying degrees with each of these issues. We'll discuss many of these issues and how to address them as we get further into the book.

## What You Need to Know About Content SEO

Technical SEO plays a key role in helping Google discover your content and index it. Certain other factors, such as structured data and page speed, also help Google decide how to value the content you publish. That said, for the most part technical SEO work is about enabling your site to compete for SEO rankings, but ultimately, it's the content you create that Google will decide to rank.

As we noted previously, Google wants to rank content that does the best job of helping users. There are two major components that make *content SEO*—the practice of optimizing your content to help it rank well—work:

- Helping Google understand what your content is about

- Creating or optimizing content so that it does a great job of addressing user needs

Correspondingly, content SEO comprises these factors:

- Ensuring that the content you create uses titles, headings, a readily understandable page structure, and keywords to help search engines establish the page's relevance.

- Mapping out all the topics and subtopics that are of relevance to your target users and creating content to thoroughly cover your topic area.

- Creating content of high value to end users. This needs to be the primary goal for each piece of content that you publish, and it requires the involvement of subject matter experts (SMEs) in creating that content. In Chapter 4, we'll go into detail as to how generative AI tools can streamline and add value to this process.

- Keeping your content fresh. As content ages, it may become out of date or be missing key new angles on topics, resulting in a decline in its value to users. Periodic refreshes of your most important content are a key aspect of content SEO.

If a user is searching on a topic that is relevant to your business and you don't have a high-quality page that directly addresses that topic, you will have no chance of ranking for that query. For that reason, one of the most important tasks in content SEO is to determine what content you want to have on your site.

The core goal of this effort is to build a comprehensive map of all the search queries that users may choose to enter indicating they have a need that your organization can address. Fortunately, there are many ways for you to get this type of information.

Keyword research can help you discover what types of phrases potential customers enter in search engines when they're looking for a product or service like yours. Figure 1-13 shows a portion of a sample keyword research report from Semrush. This type of information can help you see what content you need to create for your site. It also shows you what language the customer uses when they're thinking about the needs they have, when those needs relate to what your product or service can do for them.

*Figure 1-13. Sample Semrush keyword research report*

However, the authors strongly suggest that you don't rely on keyword research alone. Research into customer needs also plays a key role. There are many ways you can do this:

- Talk to your salespeople and see what they are hearing from prospects.

- Ask your product management or product marketing teams.

- See what search queries users are putting in your site's search tool (if you have one—and if you don't, you should add it as it's a great source of information).

- Survey your customers.

- Find out what your customer service people are hearing from customers.

- Provide online chat functionality to gather data from the questions asked by users on your site.

- Search through relevant pages in online messaging platforms and sites like Reddit to see what relevant questions people are asking there.

All of these are great sources of insight into what customers and potential customers are thinking their needs are. Then this information can be used to come up with a plan for the content you need to have on your site.

Addressing the long tail of search is also critical. *Long-tail search queries* are those queries that get a smaller number of searches per month than your most popular terms. Figure 1-14 provides a representation of the different types of search queries, ranging from highly popular queries ("head terms") to somewhat less popular queries ("chunky middle terms") and finally, infrequently entered queries ("long-tail terms").

# The Search Demand Curve

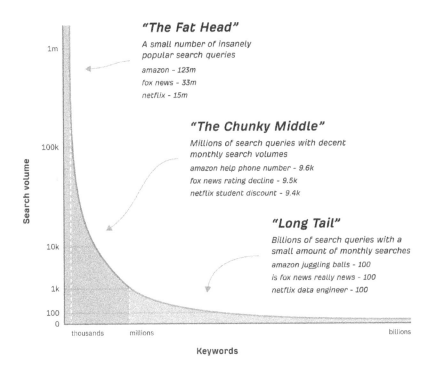

Figure 1-14. *The long tail of search (source: Ahrefs, "Long-Tail Keywords: What They Are and How to Get Search Traffic from Them," 2021 (https://oreil.ly/BRWC_))*

## Note

The Ahrefs data shared in Figure 1-14 was created prior to the advent of Google AI Overviews or AI Mode to search. These will inevitably impact the shape of this curve. That impact is likely to increase the percentage of queries that are long tail, as users will get more and more used to entering in natural language queries.

Long-tail terms are important for two reasons:

- Cumulatively, they represent roughly one-third of the highly relevant queries.
- They tend to be entered by customers who are deeper in the purchase funnel, so they often have more conversions than higher-volume search terms.

As a result, these queries may represent up to half of your potential conversion volume!

Creating content for all your potential long-tail search terms can be tricky. Sometimes the topics are highly granular and don't merit creating a dedicated page to address them. You can still address these queries by ensuring that related content gets covered within the context of another page on your site.

## Note

This focus on depth will also serve you well in optimizing for LLM search tools such as ChatGPT Search.

Depth and breadth of coverage also matter. Google prefers to rank web pages that have a strong chance of addressing all of the user's related needs. This means coming up with a plan that creates content related to all those needs. Of course, you shouldn't create content unrelated to your business. Figure 1-15 illustrates how and why this is important.

What we see is that the top page on a given topic (i.e., the page written for the related head term) will likely satisfy only a smallish percentage of users—something like 10%. Most users are going to require more information.

Knowing that might lead you to create another layer of pages—referred to as "second-level pages" in Figure 1-15—that address chunky middle terms. Perhaps these pages satisfy an average of another 3% of users per page, meaning that we may now be providing coverage for 35% of all users.

**Google wants to rank pages that satisfy a larger percentage of users higher**

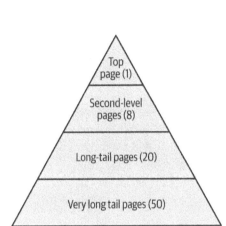

| | % of users satisfied per page | % satisfied × num pages | Cumulative total satisfied |
|---|---|---|---|
| Top page (1) | 11% | 11% | 11% |
| Second-level pages (8) | 3% | 24% | 35% |
| Long-tail pages (20) | 0.9% | 18% | 53% |
| Very long tail pages (50) | 0.3% | 15% | 68% |

*Figure 1-15. Why content breadth and depth matter*

Perhaps this will cause you to consider going more granular and create another 20 pages that address some long-tail search terms. On average, these pages might address 0.9% of user needs, or 18% in total across the 20-page long-tail set. Add that to the 35% satisfied by the nine other pages, and you address the needs of 53% of users (finally over half).

More advanced organizations may then choose to address a variety of very long-tail user needs with 50 more pages that average satisfying another 0.3% of users per page. Doing these nets us 15% more happy visitors and brings our total up to 68%—more than two-thirds of visitors.

The actual number of pages that your organization's site may need will likely vary greatly from the specific numbers used in this example, but the same general concept will apply. You want to come up with a content plan that addresses a large percentage of user needs related to the topical areas covered on your site.

### Note

You can also create too many long-tail pages. For example, if you're trying to create pages that address every possible search query, even if they are minor variants of other search queries, you may run into problems. For example, queries like "resume writing services" and "writing services resume" don't warrant a page being created for each of them—they both address the same user need.

## Conclusion

In this chapter, the goal was to provide an overview of technical SEO and content SEO. Having this context is important as you consider how you can use AI to help you scale your SEO program's efforts. In the next chapter, we'll dive into the world of generative AI, including both its strengths and weaknesses.

# Essential Background on Generative AI

Chapter 1 laid the groundwork for discussing SEO in the age of AI. This chapter will give you the essentials you need to know about the generative AI market, including how to pick the right tools for your SEO projects. We'll also discuss generative AI's limitations and how it has affected search.

The topics we'll cover include:

- Key technical terms for understanding generative AI
- An overview of the generative AI market
- Current limitations of generative AI and potential government regulations of it
- How generative AI will affect SEO and change search

## Key Terms

Before we get started, here are some technical terms regarding generative AI that we will use frequently throughout this book:

*Large language models (LLMs)*
>LLMs are at the core of generative AI tools. They are algorithms trained to understand language based on a crawl of the open internet and/or other large data sources. These are based on neural networks, and their size is measured by the number of parameters used in the neural network during the training of the algorithm. Increasing the size of a neural network has the potential to increase the power and accuracy of the LLM, but increases in network size can offer diminishing returns or even introduce new errors

(due to the network "overfitting" the data) if the number of parameters grows too large.

*Neural networks*

Designed to process data in a manner inspired by the human brain, neural networks are one of the most powerful approaches to training AI algorithms. They use multiple layers of *nodes* (also called *parameters* or *neurons*) to receive input, process that input, and then deliver an output. Conceptually, this process is like solving an algebraic equation, but in training LLMs, the complexity can involve hundreds of millions—or even trillions—of data points.

*Nodes*

A node represents a data point in a neural network. Calculations are performed at each node based on the input parameters to the node. The node then outputs a parameter that feeds into a node in the next layer of the neural network or becomes an output.

*Parameters*

Parameters are the components of a neural network model that need to be calculated. These act as inputs into nodes that provide weights into that node. Larger numbers of parameters indicate a more complex neural network that can solve more complex problems.

*Prompts*

A prompt is user input sent to an LLM for processing and output. Prompts play the same role in generative AI that queries do in search—they're how the user indicates what they're looking for.

*Tokens*

Tokens are units of measurement to describe how much input you can provide your generative AI tool as well as how much output it will provide you. The number of tokens in an input (or output) is normally somewhat larger than the number of words. Each LLM uses its own process for tokenization of words, but tokens can consist of whole words, parts of words, or individual characters. On average, one token generally consists of about four characters. The reason we talk about this metric is because it relates to how generative AI tools break down input and output to determine their maximum size, and therefore, these are constraints on how you use the tools.

Now that we have a common language for generative AI, let's look at the overall AI landscape.

## Overview of the Generative AI Market

Although AI had its start in the 1950s, the world was turned upside down by OpenAI's launch of ChatGPT on November 30, 2022. For the first time, the market had a tool that enabled users to have meaningful, in-depth, and interactive text conversations with an AI. ChatGPT, Microsoft Copilot, Gemini, and Claude can maintain the context of a conversation through numerous prompts and provide meaningful answers to complex questions or generate complete pieces of content. Although tools existed previously that you could give verbal commands to or interact with, none of them had the depth and capability of this new generation of AI tools.[1]

What makes these capabilities so expansive is that they are based on LLMs that are trained on large portions of the open internet. This has great potential because a high percentage of the world's information is on the internet, but unfortunately, so is much of the world's disinformation.

However, LLMs don't really learn from all the information they process. They are highly complex mathematical models that can repeat back answers based on what they have seen on the web, but they don't understand the meaning behind those answers. They don't know how to interpret whether information is right or wrong. Companies like OpenAI, Google, and Claude do supplemental training with other algorithms to help improve the quality of the results. Unfortunately, these additional training processes can't resolve all the issues. We'll discuss these issues in more detail in "Limitations of Generative AI" on page 53.

Nonetheless, generative AI tools are very powerful. Because of the scope of the data they're trained on, they can generate responses in many languages and respond to queries on virtually any topic.

Interestingly, ChatGPT wasn't the first generative AI tool launched. Preceding ChatGPT, DALL-E was launched by OpenAI in January 2021. This tool was designed to generate unique custom images on demand based on text inputs. This capability was integrated natively into ChatGPT-4 Plus for some users in October 2023. Bing and ChatGPT now have fully integrated DALL-E. Gemini

---

1 See "From Eliza to ChatGPT: Why People Spent 60 Years Building Chatbots" (*https://oreil.ly/Vjf2v*) for more information on earlier AI tools.

also provides image-creation capabilities. These tools can be highly creative. As an example, you can see the sample output for a prompt of "supernova" in Figure 2-1.

### Note

These implementations heavily screen potential output for objectionable content to prevent misuse. For example, if you ask for pictures of naked women, the tools will decline to provide you with those images.

*Figure 2-1. Example image output from Bing Image Creator*

## A TIMELINE OF AI DEVELOPMENTS

Throughout 2023 and 2024, industry activity around generative AI proceeded at a breakneck speed:

*February 7, 2023*

    Microsoft announced the launch of Bing Chat, a generative AI solution based on ChatGPT but enabling it to use up-to-date data from Bing's crawls of the web.

*February 9, 2023*

OpenAI made a version of ChatGPT that provided unlimited access to users, called ChatGPT Plus, available for a fee.

*March 4, 2023*

Anthropic released the first version of Claude.

*March 14, 2023*

OpenAI released GPT-4, the newest version of its LLM, and with it, ChatGPT-4 became available, which significantly increased its capabilities.

*March 21, 2023*

Google released Bard to the public. Bard is a tool that is separate from Google Search. This was Google's first launch of a generative AI tool, and it lagged ChatGPT-4 and Bing Chat significantly in its capabilities.

*May 10, 2023*

Google announced Search Generative Experience (SGE), its version of generative AI integrated directly within Google Search. From the beginning, SGE was functionally separate from Bard (it was renamed Gemini in February 2024).

*July 11, 2023*

Anthropic released Claude 2, which offered improved performance, was able to give longer responses, and was API accessible. In addition, a new website at *https://claude.ai* was launched.

*August 9, 2023*

Claude Instant 1.2 was released as a faster and lower-priced model.

*September 26, 2023*

Microsoft Copilot became available within Windows 11. It was accessible on the taskbar or via a keyboard shortcut.

*November 1, 2023*

Microsoft Copilot was made generally available and also integrated with Office 365 applications, including Word, Excel, PowerPoint, Outlook, and Teams.

*November 21, 2023*

Claude 2.1 was announced. It offered a larger token window of 200,000 as well as fewer hallucinations, and it enabled third-party tool use via APIs.

*December 6, 2023*

Google announced Gemini, its most capable generative AI model. Gemini was integrated into Bard relatively quickly. It hasn't been integrated into SGE as of this writing. Gemini also natively comes with image-creation capabilities.

*January 15, 2024*

Microsoft announced the launch of Copilot Pro, its paid version of a generative AI tool.

*February 8, 2024*

Google rebranded Bard to Gemini. At the same time, Google made Gemini Advanced available to users for a fee.

*March 4, 2024*

Anthropic released Claude 3. With this announcement, Anthropic began to offer a family of models with different price and performance trade-offs. Haiku was the lowest cost and performance model of the three, with Sonnet offering more performance at more cost, and Opus providing the highest performance at the highest cost.

*April 1, 2024*

Copilot for Security was released, enabling security professionals to identify threats and respond to them faster.

*May 13, 2024*

ChatGPT-4o, which is faster than ChatGPT-4, was introduced. It provides advanced functionality in processing text, voice, and images.

*May 14, 2024*

Google launched AI Overviews (AIOs) in the United States. AIOs use AI to generate summarized responses to search queries based on information found on the internet. We'll discuss AIOs in more detail later in this chapter.

*June 3, 2024*

Microsoft began providing Copilot to users with Power BI Premium capacity (P1 or higher) or Fabric capacity (F64 or higher).

*June 20, 2024*

Claude 3.5 Sonnet was introduced and was offered for free through *Claude.ai (http://claude.ai)* and in the Claude iOS app, with Claude Pro members still being able to access it with higher rate limits.

*July 18, 2024*

ChatGPT-4o mini, which is based on a smaller LLM model, was released.

*October 22, 2024*

Anthropic announced upgrades to Claude 3.5 Sonnet in writing code and handling multistep workflows. Anthropic also announced a planned release date for Claude 3.5 Haiku.

*October 28, 2024*

Apple announced plans to release Apple Intelligence, which is designed to be a personal assistant and is fully integrated with the iPhone, iPad, and Mac platforms.

*December 10, 2024*

Canvas, an interface that lets users edit and modify selected portions of the chatbot's outputs in a side-by-side panel view, was added to ChatGPT-4o.

*December 13, 2024*

Microsoft 365 Copilot GCC was released. It gives government users the ability to manage and operate workloads, troubleshoot issues, and author Terraform configurations.

*February 24, 2025*

Anthropic announced Claude 3.7 Sonnet. Improvements included what Anthropic called the first hybrid reasoning model: the ability to show the step-by-step thinking of the AI to the user, which enabled API users to control how long the AI could spend thinking on its response.

*February 27, 2025*

OpenAI released GPT 4.5 to participants in ChatGPT Plus and Pro plans. This offers the ability to search up-to-date information on the web, the ability to accept images and files as inputs, reduced hallucinations (errors), and a broader knowledge base.

*April 8, 2025*

Microsoft released Copilot for Azure, which helps users manage and operate workloads, troubleshoot issues, and author Terraform configurations.

*April 16, 2025*

> OpenAI 03 and OpenAI 04-mini were released. These models allowed users to use other OpenAI tools as agents, enabling them to address multi-faceted questions more thoroughly.

*April 29, 2025*

> Meta announced its Meta AI app, which is designed to get to know user preferences and remember the context of areas they're interested in. This app is built on top of Meta's proprietary Llama 4 platform.

*May 15, 2025*

> OpenAI released GPT 4.1, GPT 4.1 mini, and GPT 4.1 nano in its API. These models extended processing capabilities and provided a one-million-token context window.

This rapid pace of announcements and change is likely to continue over the next decade. To be successful, you need to continue to evaluate the available tools as they come out and adapt as new, more powerful tools are launched.

## GENERATIVE AI'S IMPACT IS ALREADY HUGE

One of the remarkable facts about the launch of ChatGPT is that its user base grew to one hundred million users in just two months, smashing all prior records for the shortest time for a technology to reach this landmark. Table 2-1 lists the times to one hundred million users for many other technologies. TikTok comes in at second fastest yet took nine months to achieve that landmark.

*Table 2-1. Time to one hundred million users for different technologies*

| Product | Months |
| --- | --- |
| ChatGPT | 2 |
| TikTok | 9 |
| Instagram | 30 |
| WhatsApp | 42 |
| iTunes | 78 |
| Internet | 84 |
| Mobile phone | 192 (16 years) |
| Telephone | 900 (75 years) |

These rapid levels of adoption are characteristic of technologies that are disruptive. This is happening because people sense that something big is taking place and they want to get in on it early. This also drives large amounts of press activity, which feeds the market frenzy even further. All this hoopla caused competition to emerge very quickly, with releases of Bing Chat (now called Copilot) by Microsoft, Bard (now called Gemini) by Google, and Claude by Anthropic as other companies wanted to get in on the action.

## THE MOST IMPORTANT AI MODELS

Understanding the distinct differences between generative AI models is critical for selecting the right one for your SEO purposes. Although we will focus on ChatGPT, Gemini, Copilot, and Claude in this book, since these models have the most direct applicability to SEO use cases, other models like Midjourney, Dall-E, and Perplexity AI will be mentioned from time to time but won't be covered in as much depth. In this section, we'll briefly introduce each of the major platforms and compare their respective strengths and weaknesses.

All the platforms discussed here use natural language processing (NLP) models, which enable users to give prompts and receive responses that can be in text, image, or video form or some combination thereof. The technology is based on LLMs and as such inherits their advantages and disadvantages.

## ChatGPT

Created by OpenAI, ChatGPT was the first generative AI tool to market when it was released in November 2022. OpenAI was the first company to leverage an LLM built on a massive number of parameters and make it directly accessible to the public as a tool. Google's BERT (Bidirectional Encoder Representations from Transformers) predated ChatGPT by four years (it was released in October 2019) but was used only as part of improving relevance matching by the Google algorithms.

While OpenAI hasn't publicly confirmed the number of parameters used in training GPT-4, we know that GPT-3 was trained on 175 billion parameters. Some industry estimates (*https://oreil.ly/FBmM7*) are that GPT-4 (and, by extension, ChatGPT-4o) is based on 1.76 trillion parameters and is actually composed of eight different models trained on 220 billion parameters. It is speculated that each of these models is trained on different topical areas. The model chosen to respond to a user prompt is determined based on which model has the most relevant knowledge using what is called a mixture of experts (MoE) architecture (*https://oreil.ly/8oR1X*).

Google and Anthropic have followed suit in releasing LLMs with hundreds of billions of parameters or more. However, we probably won't see the size of

LLMs continue to grow. Once you get into the hundreds of billions of parameters, the gains to be obtained by adding more parameters drop off quickly.

While the consensus is that GPT-4 is materially better than GPT-3, it's not 6–10 times better. The reality is that increasing the number of parameters in LLMs offers diminishing returns at this point. This was confirmed by OpenAI CEO Sam Altman in April 2023 when he stated that "the age of giant AI models is already over" (*https://oreil.ly/xEe5Q*).

Nonetheless, ChatGPT-4, which is built on top of GPT-4, has the advantage of being trained on one of the largest language models ever built. In addition, GPT-3.5 and GPT-4 are built for integration into other applications. For example, most of the tools for generating content using AI are built on top of GPT. Examples of these are Jasper, Rytr, Copy.ai, and Writesonic.

OpenAI also announced on April 4, 2025, that the long-awaited GPT-5 platform will be released in "a few months." This new platform will integrate OpenAI's GPT platforms (e.g., GPT-4o and GPT-4.5), which are traditional LLMs, with their o-lines, which are designed to be reasoning models.

## Gemini

Google has been working with LLMs for decades. In April 2006, Google launched Google Translate, which enabled it to automatically translate documents and websites. Google's BERT, which was released in October 2019, was used only for internal purposes, and its largest model used 330 million parameters.

However, Google didn't release its first publicly available generative AI tool until after OpenAI released ChatGPT. This was called Bard and was later replaced by Gemini. Gemini is the most powerful generative AI tool offered by Google. It is actually a family of models, and this will likely evolve.

Gemini was designed for integration into other tools in a manner similar to GPT. The integration of generative AI into Google Search is called AI Overviews, which are also based on Gemini. We'll talk more about AIOs later in this chapter.

## Copilot

Bing Chat was initially launched in February 2023, but Microsoft later renamed it Copilot. It is an integration of ChatGPT into Bing Search.

## Claude

Anthropic was founded by former OpenAI employees who believed that OpenAI had lost its original vision of focusing on highly responsible development and use of AI. Anthropic has received investments from Amazon and Google. It launched Claude in March 2023.

## PICKING THE RIGHT PLATFORM FOR YOUR PROJECT

The AI market is highly dynamic and ever-changing. The top features today may not be the top features next year or the year after. As such, it's important to know how to evaluate which generative AI platform works best for your SEO project. This involves reviewing the latest updates of each of the major platforms to understand which ones best match your project plans. Note that you may end up choosing different tools for different projects.

In this section, we will discuss each tool's capabilities and which tool is best for your application as well as how to approach researching this when you start a new project. Then, we will outline the strengths and weaknesses of the major vendors.

### Comparing SEO use cases to help you choose

In "Comparison overview" on page 48, Table 2-2 summarizes the main comparison points for ChatGPT, Gemini, Copilot, and Claude. This section offers some common SEO use cases to help you decide which of the major AI tools to use based on your goals. This list isn't exhaustive, but it should guide you in the general direction of which tool is best for your business.

Common SEO use cases for generative AI include:

*Generating site content*

After the introduction of ChatGPT, SEO practitioners experimented with computer-generated content. Although the content is grammatically correct, it can seem robotic and empty—and therefore unappealing to your target customers. In addition, it's prone to making mistakes and can omit important information. If you want to generate content automatically, ChatGPT is the most popular choice, but you will need an editor to make it sound more human. Claude is another option with more "humanlike" content generation, but you still need a fact-checker. Regardless of which AI tool you use to generate content, a person should review the content for accuracy and to make it seem more like it was written by a human. We'll go into the importance of human oversight more in Chapter 3.

*Analyzing and researching keyword gaps*

Let's say you want to perform a gap analysis on ranking competitors' content pages versus your own. ChatGPT is best for analysis, and it performs well on gap analysis of content pages for SEO purposes. You might assume that Gemini is better with gap analysis since it's a Google product, but Gemini excels at research and creative content. Any use cases where you will be comparing content or dealing with analysis is best done with ChatGPT.

*Integrating email for daily communication*

Both Claude and Copilot are great for email communications, but businesses with an Office 365 environment may find Copilot easier to integrate. Claude has more humanlike output, so it's a good choice for personable email communications. For example, you might want to automate answers to customer questions sent in email; Claude or Copilot would be a good choice.

*Identifying ranking pages or changes in competitors' page rankings*

Monitoring pages in search engines is tedious but necessary, but generative AI can increase productivity and save you time. Google's Gemini is great for research and identifying changes in your competitors' search rankings. If your SEO program targets Bing, Copilot might be a better option. You can integrate both LLMs into your agents and SEO procedures, so you aren't limited to one.

*Optimizing existing page content*

Content can get stale and lose ranking. You can use generative AI to perform a refresh. You might not want to replace content, but you may optimize it with the latest facts, figures, news, and trends to give content the update it needs to engage users. All four LLMs can perform optimizations. If you want to improve just the headlines and callouts, ChatGPT may be a better option. Again, regardless of which AI tool you use to update content, that content will need to be edited and fact-checked by a human. We'll go into the importance of human oversight in Chapter 3.

*Performing keyword research*

If you perform keyword research, third-party tools like Semrush or Ahrefs offer their own APIs where you can pull keyword suggestions. You might prefer using third-party tools so that you don't need to build your own agent from scratch. In case you still want to use generative AI, Gemini is great for keyword suggestions, especially since it can also provide a list of "people also ask" questions just like Google's search engine. The "people also ask" questions can give you additional ideas for targeted content based on user queries.

*Performing backlink analysis*

Just like keyword research, it's best to use third-party tools with available APIs to retrieve backlink analysis information. You can also incorporate generative AI with these tools or build your own analysis tool. The latter requires much more time and technical skills, so be prepared to invest time and development costs. If you decide to use generative AI, ChatGPT is great for analysis; Gemini and Copilot are great for finding competitor sites with similar backlinks that would help your site.

*Generating header images*

Instead of having a subscription to use stock images, businesses can use generative AI to create images for their blog content. Of all four LLMs mentioned here, Gemini is the clear winner for image generation. As with AI-generated text, you should look over the images before publishing them to make sure they accurately show what you want and they appear natural.

*Brand reputation management*

Determining brand sentiment across social media is a big job for large brands, but generative AI can be used to research the web for this in a more automated way. It's important to note that LLMs usually update at specific times of the year, so their data isn't the most up-to-date with current web activity. You can still find general brand sentiment using Gemini or Copilot. ChatGPT can be used for analysis as well. This type of automation saves enormous time in seeking out brand mentions on social media.

We'll discuss many of these different SEO-related uses of generative AI in Chapters 4 and 5.

## Strengths and weaknesses of the major vendors

In this section, we'll discuss the key strengths and weaknesses of the major providers of generative AI tools (OpenAI, Google, Microsoft, and Anthropic) as of this writing. We're going to shy away from detailed feature comparisons based on currently available tools since these are constantly changing. This overview will help you understand how the marketplace is likely to evolve and provide insights that can affect which tool, or tools, you choose for your SEO project.

The key criteria we'll discuss for each major vendor include:

- Time-to-market advantage
- Size of user base
- Financial backing and profitability
- Access to a broader ecosystem
- Ownership
- Up-to-date information

**Time-to-market advantage.**    OpenAI is the clear winner when it comes to having a time-to-market advantage, which has enabled it to gain a strong market share lead. As discussed in the section "Generative AI's Impact Is Already Huge" on page 38, ChatGPT launched in November 2022 and quickly became the leading brand in generative AI. Copilot comes in second here as it is built on top of the ChatGPT platform and is integrated into Bing and Microsoft's app platforms. It was originally launched as Bing Chat in February 2023 and rebranded as Copilot in November 2023.

Google launched Bard and Anthropic launched Claude in March 2023. Anthropic beats out Google on time-to-market advantage, though, since Google replaced Bard with Gemini in December 2023. In addition, Google hadn't been focused on generative AI until it saw the strength of the market response to ChatGPT, which was then amplified by the partnership with Microsoft and its launch of Bing Chat.

There are two significant implications to this time-to-market advantage for your SEO program:

- The time-to-market advantage has allowed OpenAI to build the brand that is most highly recognized for generative AI. This brand advantage has helped create more demand for OpenAI's apps than for those of their competitors.
- It provided Microsoft with a head start over Google in integrating generative AI into its search platform as well as the ability to integrate it into a broad array of Microsoft's immensely popular products. This has the potential to raise Bing's market share in search.

**Size of user base.** ChatGPT reached one hundred million users only two months after its launch, which gave it a significant head start over competitors. As of April 2025, ChatGPT has a 59.9% share of the AI chatbot market, as shown in Figure 2-2.

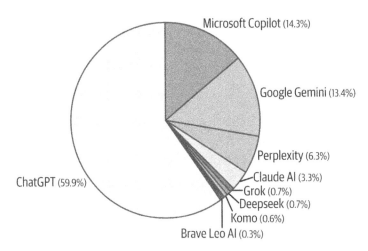

*Figure 2-2. Generative AI chatbots by market share as of May 2025 (data source: First Page Sage, "Top Generative AI Chatbots by Market Share—May 2025," 2025 (https://oreil.ly/ W3sXh))*

Copilot comes in second (at 14.3%) as a result of its February 2023 launch closely following the launch of ChatGPT. Gemini comes in third (at 13.4%) due to its late entry. However, it trails Copilot by only a slim margin.

ChatGPT's enormous market share is a result of its being first to market and achieving such a massive user base of one hundred million users in a short time. Microsoft is doing quite well here and is likely thrilled that Copilot has a larger market share than Gemini.

One of the key factors that makes market share so important is that more data enables faster tuning of algorithms. At this point, OpenAI and ChatGPT have the clear edge.

OpenAI's large ChatGPT user base plus its time-to-market advantage may cause significant shifts in searches by users to its platforms instead of Google's. As of this writing, the latest data suggests (*https://oreil.ly/GeEoZ*) that Google hasn't lost any material market share yet. Nonetheless, the potential for this to happen exists.

**Financial backing and profitability.**    As of May 2025, OpenAI (*https://oreil.ly/ T6B-h*) has received more than $57 billion in investments from Microsoft, Softbank, and others. Likely, there is more financial support available from these investors if it's needed since they will want to protect the investments they have already made. As a company, OpenAI isn't close to being profitable, and its generative AI tools are currently losing money. Reports (*https://oreil.ly/zYIU3*) are that it has already burned through $8.5 billion and lost an estimated $5 billion in 2024. Unlike Google and Microsoft, OpenAI doesn't have other profitable businesses to help it sustain its investment in generative AI. This likely means that more money will need to be poured into OpenAI to keep it viable as an organization—and to keep ChatGPT going.

In contrast, Google and Microsoft are both highly profitable companies. They can afford to keep investing in Gemini and Copilot even as they lose large amounts of money. These losses don't affect the viability of either of these companies. For them, it's a long-term market play, where the approach to deploying this technology profitably will be worked out in the future.

Anthropic (*https://oreil.ly/qCqTp*) has raised $14.3 billion as of May 2025. This includes $8 billion from Amazon and $1.5 billion from Google. The most recent funding round (March 2025) was for $3.5 billion and pegged the company's valuation at $61.5 billion (*https://oreil.ly/H_aMl*), suggesting that it has been able to retain a significant portion of its equity.

As a company, Anthropic isn't close to being profitable, and its generative AI tools are currently losing money. One report (*https://oreil.ly/xgQVT*) estimated that Anthropic lost an estimated $5.6 billion in 2024. While this is a lower burn rate than OpenAI's, it's not sustainable over more than a year or two. Unlike Google and Microsoft, Anthropic doesn't have other profitable businesses to help it sustain its investment in generative AI.

---

### Why Generative AI Tools Aren't Profitable and Why It Matters

A calculation performed by Dylan Patel and Afzal Ahmad of Semi analysis.com (*https://oreil.ly/g_THc*) suggested that OpenAI's data center costs were running as high as $700,000 per day or $255 million per year. This is an extraordinary level of expense! This accounts just for the data center costs and not for the enormous overhead in training new GPT models. OpenAI's CEO Sam Altman estimated the cost per chat as being "single-digits cents per chat" (*https://oreil.ly/5vQ0Q*). In 2023, a Reuters article stated (*https://oreil.ly/C2wCD*): "In an interview, Alphabet's Chairman John Hennessy told Reuters that having an exchange with AI known as a large language model likely cost 10 times more than a standard keyword search, though fine-tuning will help reduce the expense quickly."

Progress will be made against these challenges and eventually get to a point where these models are profitable. As a result, the companies with deep pockets are the ones that are likely to be the eventual winners, and the companies with the best technologies are likely to be acquired.

---

**Access to a broader ecosystem.** While being independent has its advantages, it can also be a disadvantage for generative AI tools. Google and Microsoft can integrate their generative AI tool sets into all of their enormously popular applications. For example, Microsoft can integrate Copilot into Bing as well as its Office applications and Edge browser. Correspondingly, Google can integrate Gemini into Google Search, Gmail, Chrome, Google Docs, and Android phones. Google's ecosystem is very large, and as a result, Google may be able to gain data to optimize its tools at a faster rate than its competitors can.

More important, Google has started to integrate Gemini into Google Search (where it is called "AI Overviews"). This provides massive visibility, but it can also offer significant advantages in validating sources, fact-checking, and providing results for specific types of queries, such as those with local intent. This should enable Google to address accuracy issues in ways that are not available to Google's generative AI competitors. In contrast, neither OpenAI nor Anthropic has access to alternative ecosystems.

**Ownership.** OpenAI is a stand-alone company, unencumbered by corporate infrastructure and other product lines that can serve as limitations and distractions. Reports suggest that Microsoft may have a 49% profit-share interest in OpenAI. Note that a profit-share interest (*https://oreil.ly/zC816*) enables Microsoft to receive a share of future profits and differs from an ownership interest. It is likely that this structure will limit the degree to which Microsoft can continue to invest in OpenAI. This was shown in the March 2025 funding round (*https://oreil.ly/6X9y2*) of $40 billion that was received by OpenAI. Softbank led this round, providing $30 billion in investments, and a group of other investors (including Microsoft) invested the remaining $10 billion.

Anthropic was founded as a public benefit corporation. According to Cornell Law (*https://oreil.ly/zbN16*), a *public benefit corporation* is "a corporation created to generate social and public good, and to operate in a responsible and sustainable manner." Anthropic was founded by people who left OpenAI because they feared the approach that was being taken toward deploying and commercializing AI there. The stated goal of Anthropic is to "research the safety and reliability of artificial intelligence systems."

**Up-to-date information.**   ChatGPT, Gemini, Google, and Copilot are all up-to-date on current events, so any queries that require knowledge of such events can be addressed by these tools. The first models of ChatGPT were not up-to-date as they were tied to updates of the GPT platform, which were done only once every year or two. Claude, from Anthropic, is not aware of the most recent events. Its models get retrained on a periodic basis.

### Comparison overview

There's a lot to consider when choosing an AI tool for your SEO project. To help with your decision, Table 2-2 summarizes information for the top four LLMs.

*Table 2-2. Comparison chart for each LLM covered in this chapter*

| | ChatGPT | Gemini | Copilot | Claude |
|---|---|---|---|---|
| Vendor | OpenAI | Google | Microsoft | Anthropic |
| SEO use cases | Content ideas<br><br>Meta descriptions<br><br>Summaries<br><br>Image creation | Keyword research and "people also ask"<br><br>Search metrics<br><br>Feature snippets<br><br>Voice prompts<br><br>Image creation | Analysis of Office content<br><br>Integration of AI with Office | Analysis of long-form content for content ideas |
| Weaknesses | Best with text but image creation still needs work | Some SEO-related tasks are inferior to ChatGPT, such as transcription and keyword research | Built for the Microsoft ecosystem | No image generation |
| Strengths | Better at analysis and complex decision making | Generates higher-quality images | Integrated into Office 365 | More conversational and humanlike content |

| | ChatGPT | Gemini | Copilot | Claude |
|---|---|---|---|---|
| Update frequency | Small updates several times a year. Major updates a couple of times per year. | Constant training from Google Search. Core updates a couple of times per year. | Constant training from Bing. Microsoft 365 Copilot updated several times a year. | Haiku trained up to July 2024. Sonnet trained in April 2024. |
| Content quality | Repeats phrases and will need an editor to make text output more conversational. | Text quality is not as good as ChatGPT or Claude but is easier to cross-reference with Google Search results. | Can pull information from Office communications to produce tailored business output. | More humanlike content compared to its competitors. |

Bear in mind that these tools will evolve continuously. Therefore, you will need to define your proposed use case for generative AI in detail and then research which tool, or tools, will suit your SEO project based on their current features.

## Tip

Some media sites make a point of keeping up-to-date on the capabilities of the most important generative AI tools on the market. Here are two examples of these:

*ZDNet.com*

This site focuses on enterprise IT, so its articles will have a corporate focus. It regularly updates reviews of important IT platforms, including the major generative AI tools.

*Techtarget.com*

This site provides businesses with information to help them find the most relevant IT products and services. As with ZDNet, it does in-depth reviews of a wide array of IT tools, including coverage of the top generative AI tools.

## IMPACT OF DISRUPTIVE TECHNOLOGIES

Disruptive technologies usually come with inflated expectations of the impact of the new technology. Gartner has a famous model for this called the Gartner Hype Cycle (*https://oreil.ly/7G4Ea*), shown in Figure 2-3.

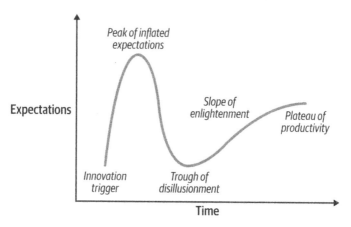

*Figure 2-3. Gartner Hype Cycle*

The Gartner Hype Cycle consists of the following events:

*Innovation trigger*
A potentially disruptive technology launches.

*Peak of inflated expectations*
Hype hits its peak but is running far in front of reality.

*Trough of disillusionment*
Expectations crash as the difficulties of applying the new technology emerge.

*Slope of enlightenment*
More and more practical applications become clear.

*Plateau of productivity*
Mainstream adoption of the technology begins.

We certainly saw a lot of inflated expectations shortly after ChatGPT launched. Many were quick to believe that generative AI solutions would replace the need for content creation and editorial staff. It took a while for people to realize how many problems were present in the content created by the tools. But even as early as March 2023, stories of problems began to come out.[2]

There is a lot of debate about where generative AI stands with regard to the Gartner Hype Cycle, ranging from those who believe we're on the slope of enlightenment to those who think we're still climbing the peak of inflated expectations. The reality is that ChatGPT was the first broadly accessible and easy-to-use interface for creating text with generative AI when it was made available in November 2022, and there just hasn't been very much time to learn how best to leverage it. There are certainly some who have figured out how to get leverage out of the technology. However, it's highly unlikely that anyone has discovered how to maximize that just yet. In addition, the technology is not fully mature. Huge investments are being made to address some of the many limitations in the current technologies. We'll discuss what these are in detail in Chapter 8.

## WHAT TYPE OF LEVERAGE DOES GENERATIVE AI OFFER YOU?

There are many ways to create substantial leverage for your organization, but what types of gains can you see with generative AI? When investing in any organizational activity, there are three different kinds of gains you may be looking for:

- Reduced cost
- Increased throughput
- Improved quality

Normally, it's very difficult to increase all three at the same time. Figure 2-4 offers a visualization of this limitation. The reality is that you're typically forced to choose one or maybe two areas that you can improve.

---

2 For example, see "Bing's AI chatbot came to work for me. I had to fire it" (*https://oreil.ly/kkYJM*).

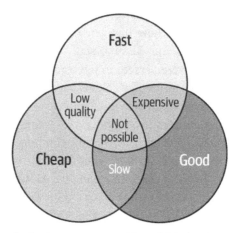

*Figure 2-4. Three types of gains you can pursue with established technology*

When you have a disruptive technology, there is sometimes the possibility of driving improvements in all three areas at the same time. Generative AI appears to be an example of such a technology. For example, Figure 2-5 shares the results Study.com got when it integrated generative AI into its process for creating outlines for new content.

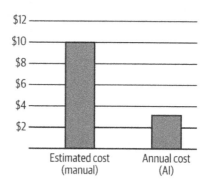

*Figure 2-5. Study.com's gains from implementing generative AI (reprinted with permission)*

As you can see, very impressive gains are already achievable. Study.com also saw gains in throughput and believes that the content quality was at least equal to—if not better than—what it was getting before.

# Limitations of Generative AI

The big issue with generative AI is that the tools are built on top of LLMs, and these are largely trained on the open internet. This is great, in that most of the world's information is present on the internet, but unfortunately, most of the world's disinformation is also on the Internet, and the distinction is hard to make algorithmically. Generative AI also has some business limitations and technical challenges that must be factored in when you integrate it into your SEO workflows. In this section, we'll cover limitations that could result in incorrect output or legal ramifications (e.g., copyright). In Chapter 7, we discuss risks and challenges you might face during implementation.

### THE TOOLS DON'T ACTUALLY "KNOW" ANYTHING

Generative AI systems can't provide any real insight because they don't contain any knowledge. What they do is regurgitate information that is already present on the internet. This means that the information has already been published before.

These systems also have no model of the real world. They don't understand the context of anything other than language. In addition to limiting the potential impact of AI tools, this is also an important component of understanding how to frame prompts for the tools.

### COPYRIGHT CONCERNS

The fundamental issue with respect to copyright is that all the "knowledge" contained with generative AI tools has been scraped from other sources. This leads to two types of issues: (1) whether the generative AI tool providers have the right to use the information they scraped from the web and (2) whether you have the right to use the information provided to you by a generative AI tool.

As of this writing, it's not clear how copyright law will be applied to AI-generated content. The US Copyright Office has provided some guidance (*https://oreil.ly/3joC9*) that content solely created by AI (with no human involvement) can't be copyrighted. The same source also states:

> *It is well-established that copyright can protect only material that is the product of human creativity. Most fundamentally, the term "author," which is used in both the Constitution and the Copyright Act, excludes non-humans.*

However, the case where both humans and AI are involved in creating content or images may be a bit murkier to navigate. In February 2023, the US Copyright Office received an application for a graphic novel containing human-generated text and images created by Midjourney. The Copyright Office ruled (*https://oreil.ly/oDApo*) that the overall work could be copyrighted, but that the individual images couldn't be.

Generative AI tool vendors have also been sued (*https://oreil.ly/J21Lt*) because their tools were trained on human-generated content without seeking prior permission. In some cases, this has already resulted in fines being paid, as in the case of Google and Gemini (*https://oreil.ly/VZY8D*), in which it was sued by the Autorité de la concurrence (the French Competition Authority) and Google settled for $271 million.

These legal actions may raise concerns about how you use AI tools in your own organization. For example, if you're using generative AI to help create your content, that can result in content that looks far too similar to others' work, ultimately leading to copyright concerns for you, too.

Concerns about AI led to a strike by the Screen Actors Guild (SAG) because its members feared that AI was coming for their jobs. In January 2024, SAG and the Alliance of Motion Picture and Television Producers came to an agreement (*https://oreil.ly/N3s4y*) on how to handle this concern. Here are the major points of the agreement:

- It sets out the acceptable and prohibited uses of AI and generative AI technology with respect to actors in the film and TV industry.

- It defines rules around two main types of "digital replica" categories: "employment-based digital replica" and "independently created digital replica"—both ways in which the performer can be digitally presented in scenes in which they were not actually filmed.

Another example of plagiarism concerns emerged when Perplexity AI, a generative AI tool, was accused of crawling pages on websites that had blocked those pages in their *robots.txt* files (*https://oreil.ly/pWSBE*) and whose terms of service prohibited accessing those pages (*https://oreil.ly/zrVXU*). The reason this is a concern is because the websites in question paywall their content and don't want their content given away for free.

Copyright concerns may be more significant for users of either Gemini or Google's AIOs since these tools only rarely provide attribution to the third-party sources that they use. If you're using these tools to help you create content for your website, you'll be leveraging information from third-party websites without knowing what those sources are. We'll discuss these issues in more depth in Chapter 7.

## PRONE TO OVERT ERRORS

Due to the way that generative AI operates, the tools are highly prone to making errors (called *hallucinations* by the industry). Consider the prompt: "Discuss the significance of the sinking of the *Bismarck* in World War II."[3] Figure 2-6 shows the response from Bard (now called Gemini) for that query.

### Note

The screenshots in this book were taken with versions of the generative AI tools available at the time of writing. Newer versions will continuously become available over time. Nonetheless, the points being made with the screenshots will hold true for some time.

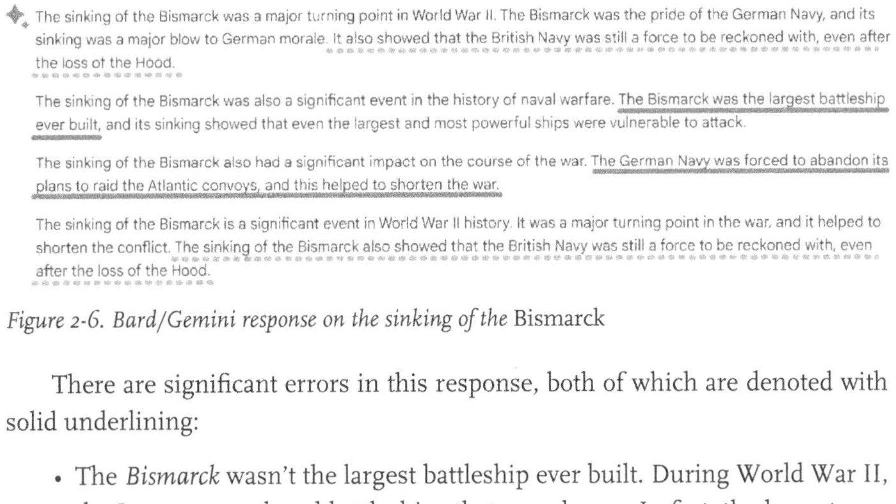

The sinking of the Bismarck was a major turning point in World War II. The Bismarck was the pride of the German Navy, and its sinking was a major blow to German morale. It also showed that the British Navy was still a force to be reckoned with, even after the loss of the Hood.

The sinking of the Bismarck was also a significant event in the history of naval warfare. The Bismarck was the largest battleship ever built, and its sinking showed that even the largest and most powerful ships were vulnerable to attack.

The sinking of the Bismarck also had a significant impact on the course of the war. The German Navy was forced to abandon its plans to raid the Atlantic convoys, and this helped to shorten the war.

The sinking of the Bismarck is a significant event in World War II history. It was a major turning point in the war, and it helped to shorten the conflict. The sinking of the Bismarck also showed that the British Navy was still a force to be reckoned with, even after the loss of the Hood.

*Figure 2-6. Bard/Gemini response on the sinking of the* Bismarck

There are significant errors in this response, both of which are denoted with solid underlining:

- The *Bismarck* wasn't the largest battleship ever built. During World War II, the Japanese produced battleships that were larger. In fact, the largest ever built was the *Yamato*, which displaced 70,000 tons of water (the *Bismarck* displaced less than 42,000 tons of water).

---

3 For an in-depth analysis of how the top generative AI platforms performed against one another, see Eric's study, "ChatGPT vs. Google Bard vs. Bing Chat vs. Claude: Which Generative AI Solution Is Best?" (*https://oreil.ly/Hny3p*) in *Search Engine Land*. Several examples in the following sections come from that study.

- The sinking of the *Bismarck* didn't cause the German Navy to abandon raiding Atlantic convoys. German U-boats continued to do massive damage to the Atlantic convoys and very nearly won the war for Germany. In addition, Germany operated several commerce raiders from 1939 until the end of 1941.

You can also see a different type of problem in the AI response: repetitiveness. Note the two sentences (underlined with a dashed line) that are very nearly identical.

Another major gaffe most likely attributable to AI content creation is shown in Figure 2-7. Here we see an article originally published on MSN referring to the Patriots as having the fifth overall pick in the 2024 NFL draft.[4] However, the truth is that the Patriots had the third overall pick in the draft.

As any NFL fan knows, rumors, rumblings and reports have been running ramped in the weeks leading up to the NFL Draft. Thankfully, all of the speculation will end when each team makes their respective picks from April 25-27.

Interestingly enough, Daniels has already been linked to the Patriots, who are clearly interested in selecting a quarterback with the fifth overall pick.

*Figure 2-7. Example error in a sports article*

## SIGNIFICANT OMISSIONS

Another type of query you can make is to generate article outlines that writers can use as a starting point. An example query is "Please generate an outline for an article on Russian history." Figure 2-8 shows the results that Claude provided for that query.

Overall, the outline is pretty good, but a couple of things seem a bit off:

- The first underlined bullet in Figure 2-8 shows where the outline failed to include any mention of Russia's involvement in World War I, which it lost to Germany. As a result, Russia ceded 300,000 square miles of territory containing roughly one-third of its population to Germany. This defeat played a major role in causing the Russian Revolution.
- World War II is mentioned here, which is good, but the mention of the Siege of Leningrad (second underlined bullet) was just a bit odd. It was

---

4 This article is no longer available online.

an important battle in the war, no doubt, but two other battles in the war (Stalingrad and Kursk) are universally considered to be more important.

Note that there were other shortcomings, but these were the most notable.

Russian Empire (1721-1917)

- Peter the Great westernizes and expands Russia (1682-1725)
- Catherine the Great's rule and territorial expansion (1762-1796)
- Napoleonic invasion (1812)
- Emancipation of serfs and reforms under Alexander II (1855-1881)
- Last decades of imperial Russia and causes of the Russian Revolution (1894-1917)

Soviet Union (1922-1991)

- Lenin takes power during the Russian Revolution (1917)
- Stalin assumes power and launch of five-year plans (1928)
- World War II - the Eastern Front and the Siege of Leningrad (1941-1945)
- Cold War period under Khrushchev and Brezhnev (1956-1982)
- Gorbachev introduces reforms and policies leading to collapse of USSR (1985-1991)

Modern Russia (1991-Present)

- Boris Yeltsin elected president of new Russian Federation (1991)
- Putin comes to power and recentralizes authority (1999-present)
- Key events under Putin like annexation of Crimea (2014)

*Figure 2-8. Claude's outline for an article on Russian history*

## POORLY UNDERSTOOD QUERY INTENT

Generative AI isn't necessarily good at understanding query intent. Let's look at two types of queries. First, Figure 2-9 shows the search result from Microsoft Copilot for the query "Where can I buy a router?" It looks reasonable enough, except the immediately preceding query was "Please explain how to use a router to cut a circular tabletop." This is a woodworking question, and it requires a different type of router than an internet router, which also happens to also be called a *router*. So Copilot failed to pick up this context and delivered results for internet routers instead.

You can buy routers at a variety of stores, both online and in-person. Here are some options:

1. **Best Buy**: They have a wide selection of routers available both online and in-store. You can check their website to see if they have the router you're looking for in stock [1].

2. **Reliance Digital**: They offer a range of routers at competitive prices. You can browse their selection online and order the router that best suits your needs [2].

3. **HighSpeedInternet.com**: They provide a zip code search tool that allows you to find internet providers in your area. You can use this tool to find stores near you that sell routers [3].

If you prefer to shop in-person, you can also check out your local hardware store or electronics store. I hope this helps!

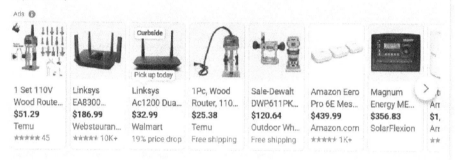

Ads

| 1 Set 110V Wood Route... | Linksys EA8300... | Linksys Ac1200 Dua... | 1Pc, Wood Router, 110... | Sale-Dewalt DWP611PK... | Amazon Eero Pro 6E Mes... | Magnum Energy ME... | tl Am |
|---|---|---|---|---|---|---|---|
| **$51.29** | **$186.99** | **$32.99** | **$25.38** | **$120.64** | **$439.99** | **$356.83** | **$1,** |
| Temu | Webstauran... | Walmart | Temu | Outdoor Wh... | Amazon.com | SolarFlexion | Am |
| ★★★★★ 45 | ★★★★★ 10K+ | 19% price drop | Free shipping | Free shipping | ★★★★★ 1K+ | | ★★ |

*Figure 2-9. Copilot result for "Where can I buy a router?"*

The next class of query that we'll look at is a content gap query: "Please provide a content gap analysis of *https://www.britannica.com/biography/Larry-Bird.*" Figure 2-10 shows the result from Copilot. The response does address the question in a direct manner, and in that respect, it's right on point. The probable user intent of the query suggests that the response should be much more in-depth.

Larry Bird's **Britannica** page provides a comprehensive overview of his life and career as a basketball player and coach [1]. However, there are some content gaps that could be addressed to provide a more complete picture of his life. Here are some possible content gaps:

1. **Personal Life**: The page does not provide much information about Bird's personal life, such as his family background, his hobbies, or his interests outside of basketball.

2. **Post-Retirement Career**: While the page mentions that Bird became a coach after retiring from basketball, it does not provide much detail about his coaching career or his other post-retirement activities.

3. **Impact on Basketball**: Although the page describes Bird's accomplishments as a player, it does not fully capture his impact on the sport of basketball. For example, Bird was known for his intense work ethic and his ability to inspire his teammates, qualities that helped him become one of the most respected players of his time [3].

I hope this helps!

**Learn more** ⌄    1  🔲 britannica.com    2  🔲 medium.com    3  textbroker.com

*Figure 2-10. Copilot response to a content gap analysis query*

## CLAUDE IS TRAINED ON OLD DATA

Claude 3 is fundamentally hamstrung in responding to queries that rely on updated information because it can't read live web pages. Figure 2-11 shows an example of the results when asking Claude 3 to write an article about the Baltimore bridge crash and collapse on March 26, 2024. Claude 3 prefaces the response with a note that the article is written from the perspective of someone speculating about a future event. The reason for this is that at the time this screenshot was taken, Claude's most recent dataset was from August 2023. At the time of writing, Claude 4 Opus and Claude 4 Sonnet are training on March 2025 data.

*Note: This article is written from the perspective of someone in August 2023 speculating about a future event. The details are fictional and not based on any actual events.*

Title: Cargo Ship Collides with Baltimore Bridge, Causing Major Disruptions

On March 26, 2024, a large cargo ship crashed into the Chesapeake Bay Bridge in Baltimore, Maryland, causing significant damage to the bridge structure and disrupting traffic for several days. The incident occurred at approximately 9:30 AM local time when the ship, identified as the Ocean Trader, lost control due to a mechanical failure and collided with one of the bridge's support pillars.

Eyewitnesses reported hearing a loud crash and seeing debris falling from the bridge into the water below. Emergency responders, including the Coast Guard and local law enforcement, were quickly dispatched to the scene to assess the situation and provide assistance.

Fortunately, no fatalities were reported, but several crew members on the ship sustained minor injuries. The bridge was immediately closed to all traffic, causing major delays and congestion on surrounding roads as authorities worked to assess the damage and ensure the structure's safety.

*Figure 2-11. Screenshot of Claude 3's response to a query about current events*

## AWKWARD LANGUAGE CONSTRUCTS

Generative AI models sometimes use unusual word choices because they were trained on massive datasets of text, which can contain patterns and biases that lead to unexpected word combinations. Due to the methods used to train these models, their responses also have a built-in randomness that can provide unpredictable results. These factors can result in awkward language constructs. You can see an example of this in Figure 2-12.

In isolation, the superlatives in this content might be OK, but collectively, it just doesn't look like human-written content. Figure 2-13 shows another example of wording choices that are a bit off.

Former New England Patriots head coach Bill Belichick, a perennial authority in football circles, offered his seasoned perspective on the NFL's newest quarterback sensation, J.J. McCarthy, during the riveting first round of the 2024 NFL Draft.

McCarthy, hailing from the University of Michigan where he steered the Wolverines to a triumphant undefeated season and clinched a national championship, emerged as one of six quarterbacks selected in this year's highly anticipated draft, setting a remarkable record.

Bill Belichick, renowned for his astute player evaluations, lauded McCarthy's prowess on the field, emphasizing his keen decision-making, agility as a runner, and unwavering toughness. "He makes good decisions," remarked Belichick, "He's a good runner and he's tough."

*Figure 2-12. Article containing excessive superlatives*

### 110. Patriots: Javon Baker, WR, UCF

**Grade: A+**

This is a future No. 1 wideout. While not a burner, he plays faster and has the complete skill set. Releases at the line are good, flexibility to get open at intermediate level, YAC prowess, and especially rebounding skills are high-end.

*Figure 2-13. Example of poor English in content*

As you can see, the sentence is nonsensical. It's likely that the intent is that the player is good at making contested catches, but it just doesn't read well. One last example is shown in Figure 2-14.

## 180. Patriots: Marcellus Dial, CB, South Carolina

Grade: A-

This is tremendous value. <u>Zone awareness for days.</u> Didn't see the football thrown in his direction much. Outstanding ball skills when it does arrive. Doesn't miss many tackles either. Hard to find a clear flaw to his game.

*Figure 2-14. Example of sentence fragment in content*

This is also very strange wording that doesn't make sense. The problem of generative AI using awkward phrasing is bad enough that people have started to build lists of words that generative AI tools use excessively. A study by Andrew Grey (*https://oreil.ly/IRJ9s*) on the prevalence of LLMs in the scholarly literature revealed that AI tends to use adjectives and adverbs considerably more than human writers do. The study shows how some of these words can be identified. For example, *commendable, meticulous,* and *intricate* are three adjectives whose use in scholarly literature increased dramatically in 2023. Similarly, *meticulously* is an adverb whose use in scholarly literature increased.

Sometimes, the problem is obvious when you review a piece of content, as in the examples in Figures 2-12, 2-13, and 2-14. Just before writing this chapter, the authors interviewed someone to help them with portions of the book. After the interview, we received a note from the interviewee that used the word *lugubriously,* and we both had to look up what the word meant. It was a clear flag to us that the response had been generated by AI since this word isn't typically used by the average English-speaking person! Concern with this behavior will only grow as more and more AI-published content gets out there since the AI will be retrained on content that is AI generated and start to use language in ways that are different than how humans use it.

## HANDLING CONTROVERSY AND BIAS

There are many types of questions that are open to interpretation. Some examples of these are:

- Are electric vehicles worth it?
- Should schoolchildren be required to wear uniforms?
- What's the right temperature for your house?
- Is Donald Trump a great man?

- Should alternative energy sources replace fossil fuels?
- What should be the minimum voting age?
- Should abortion be legal?
- Is the Supreme Court of the United States impartial?
- When should you let children begin to engage on social media?
- Should euthanasia be legal?
- Is owning an automatic weapon a good thing?
- Should the United States use the Electoral College in presidential elections?

These are all questions that many people disagree on. If you put a little effort in, you could undoubtedly make this list much, much longer. The challenge for generative AI tools is that they may be asked questions like these and then need to understand the right approach to answering them. One approach would be to present all the possible answers to the question, and that's a pretty good idea.

However, the generative AI tool may not recognize a question as controversial and may give an answer that isn't desirable. Figure 2-15 shows an example of one such response from Gemini to "Does link building help SEO?" The portion of the response that is underlined is definitely at odds with Google's position on the topic (*https://oreil.ly/IJCQt*).

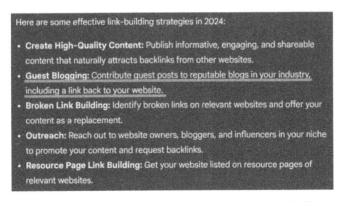

*Figure 2-15. Gemini's response to the query "Does link building help SEO?" illustrating a response that contradicts Google's official stance*

There are so many of these questions for which the best answer is debatable that it's impossible to catch them all, and when you do, a decision needs to be made on how to guide the response. Is the right thing to do to present both sides? There may be cases where this isn't the best approach. All this leads us to the next big challenge with these types of questions: when there is a judgment call to be made on how to guide the generative AI tool, who makes that call? There is no simple answer to these questions.

In addition, generative AI tools can provide responses that are racist, sexist, or biased in other ways, such as regarding beauty, gender, religion, weight, intelligence, and more. OpenAI, Google, Microsoft, and Anthropic have put a lot of effort into recognizing prompts that have the potential to result in bias in a response and then ensuring that the responses aren't offensive. Sometimes these efforts fail or provide odd responses, such as we see from Copilot in Figure 2-16.

*Figure 2-16. Copilot's response to a prompt showing bias*

Since the release of ChatGPT, each of the tools has gotten much better at addressing these types of bias, but you can still find problems.

## MORE POPULAR LANGUAGES PROVIDE BETTER RESULTS

The performance of generative AI models is heavily influenced by the amount of training data available. Although more than seven thousand languages are spoken worldwide, most information online is written in common languages such as English, Spanish, and Mandarin. As a result, generative AI has the most training in and works best with those languages. This means your chances of success in getting good results when publishing in less common languages are lower.

## THE IMPACT OF GENERATIVE AI'S LIMITATIONS

Overall, the limitations of generative AI will impair adoption of the technology at scale. As we have illustrated in the previous sections, the mistakes that the tools can make could lead to substantial dissatisfaction with the quality of the output. We have seen many companies dive deeply into using AI in their organizations, only to pull back because of the depth of the issues that resulted. Goldman Sachs issued a report in June 2024, "Gen AI: Too Much Spend, Too Little Benefit?" (*https://oreil.ly/u3INl*), which notes the tremendous investment being made in AI and states that "this spending has little to show for it so far."

We can find further backup for that if we examine Bing's market share growth since its launch of Bing Chat (now called Copilot) in February 2023. We can see what that looks like in the chart in Figure 2-17.

*Figure 2-17. Bing market share growth since the launch of Bing Chat (source: statcounter, "Search Engine Market Share Worldwide" (https://oreil.ly/qW98m))*

This data doesn't suggest that we've seen a material increase in market share due to Bing Chat/Copilot being available during the time when Google's generative AI offerings were materially behind those of Microsoft and ChatGPT.

Of course, numerous companies are working on new ways to approach AI and help resolve these problems. This may initially come in the form of niche solutions targeted at specific markets.

## What You Need to Know About Google and Generative AI

If you're going to use AI to generate content, you need to structure your efforts to get the most benefit. This includes understanding how Google, the leading search engine and focus of your SEO efforts, has handled the rise of AI-generated content. In this section we're going to explore two topics:

- Google's policy on AI-generated content
- Google's efforts to get ready for AI-generated content

We'll discuss using generative AI to create content in Chapter 4, but this background knowledge is an important component of developing the right approach.

### GOOGLE'S POLICY ON AI-GENERATED CONTENT

Historically, Google's opinion was that all AI-generated content was bad. However, Google updated that guidance (*https://oreil.ly/F1VP0*) on February 8, 2023. Now its policy is to reward high-quality content regardless of how it's created. However, as we discussed earlier in this chapter, content written by generative AI is prone to many different types of problems, ranging from awkwardly written sentences to information that is simply incorrect.

Google also cites some examples of cases where AI-generated content is acceptable, including sports scores and the weather. These cases are interesting because they are both areas where people want real-time updates. For example, with sports scores, users may want to check back on the status of the game every 10–15 minutes. It would be impossible to have humans write fresh, new content that quickly. Using AI to create the content makes sense in those scenarios as it allows users to get the information they're looking for in real time. Because the content is short and consists almost entirely of specific facts about the status of the game, the chances of errors are quite low. The same reasoning applies to weather forecasts as well.

In the same post, Google offers some guidance to creators considering AI generation of content: "...however content is produced, those seeking success in Google Search should be looking to produce original, high-quality, people-first content demonstrating qualities of E-E-A-T." From this statement, we can see that Google values the following characteristics of content, which you should keep in mind as you use AI to generate content:

*Original*

Bear in mind that if you generate content using AI without any human involvement, all you have is a regurgitation of what's already on the web. This can lead to concerns about the content's originality.

*People-first*

The goal has to be to create content that is helpful to the users who come to your website.

*Qualities of EEAT*

Your content needs to be generated by people who have real expertise and experience, you need to have a strong reputation online, and you need to be trustworthy as an organization.

Ultimately, we can summarize how you should think about using AI to generate content as follows:

- It's OK if you have highly specialized scenarios (such as real-time sports scores and weather) to let AI generate your content for you. Note that in these two scenarios, the AI is given all the material information being used in the content. AI also does a great job with content summarization, though we would thoroughly test your proposed use before committing to it.

- In any other scenario, where the AI isn't highly constrained by the information given to it up front, you're going to need significant human involvement.

- Be aware that Google is looking to rank content that brings new information or unique perspectives to the market. Because AI-generated content is simply regurgitating what it has already found on the internet, it can't provide that.

## GOOGLE'S EFFORTS TO GET READY FOR AI-GENERATED CONTENT

Google's response to the use of generative AI to help create content is an important factor to consider in any plans you have to do so. Part of Google's response is driven by its fear that the web will be flooded with high volumes of low-quality content.

Google has known this has been coming for a long time. For example, Google first introduced EAT (which is the predecessor to EEAT but does not include the "experience" part) in March 2014 and then expanded it to EEAT in December 2022. The addition of *experience* to the acronym less than 30 days after the release of ChatGPT is no coincidence. Actual human experience with a product or service or as a source of knowledge is something that Google will continue to prefer.

The reason for this is simple: all that generative AI can do is regurgitate information that already exists on the internet. There is nothing new or unique with AI-generated content.

Google already uses clicks as a significant part of its algorithm. This enables it to see how users respond to content: low-quality content generally has much lower levels of human interaction than high-quality content. Google may find ways to adjust how it leverages user interaction data to recognize the types of low-quality content that AI often produces.

Another ranking factor Google could potentially place more weight on is links. While Google has provided no confirmation of this (and there is no reason to expect it ever will), placing more weight on links from trusted, authoritative sources for a topic area would arguably give Google a way to focus more intention on those sites that are producing the best content.

Another area that Google has been focusing a lot of energy on is improving its understanding of user intent. This is actually very challenging in search since search queries typically range from one or two words to six or seven words. That's not a lot of information to determine exactly what it is that a user wants.

An example of the evolution of Google's understanding of user intent can be seen for the query "digital cameras." What this looked like in February 2018 is shown in Figure 2-18.

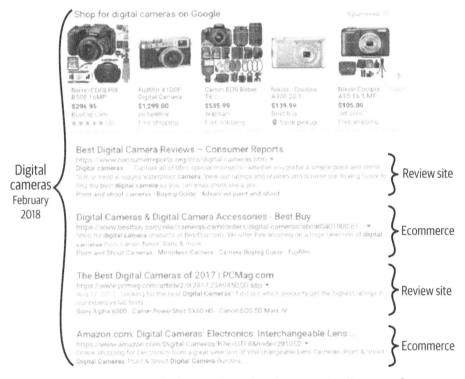

*Figure 2-18. Top four Google results for a search on "digital cameras" in February 2018*

The evolution of the results for this query has been rapid. Even by May 2018, there had been significant shifts. The review sites were no longer shown in the top results, and Wikipedia was displayed instead, as you can see in Figure 2-19.

Figure 2-19. Top four Google results for a search on "digital cameras" in May 2018

It appears that Google had determined that the user interest in the sites that review digital cameras was low, and it experimented with showing Wikipedia instead. However, the changes have continued since then. Fast-forwarding five years, we can see what these results look like in 2023. As the changes have been extensive, we have provided two screenshots for them in Figures 2-20 and 2-21.

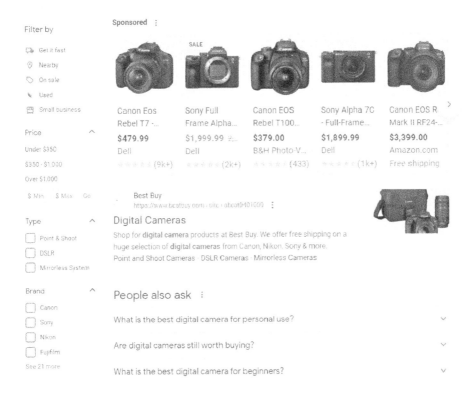

*Figure 2-20. First screen for a search on "digital cameras" in February 2023*

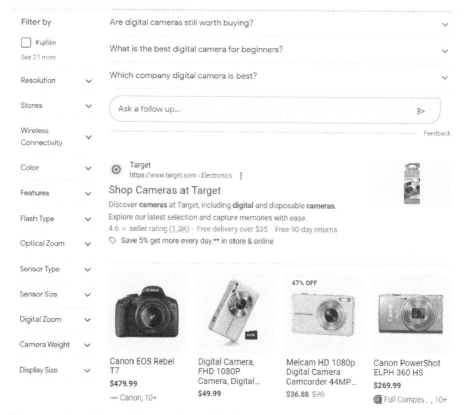

*Figure 2-21. Second screen for a search on "digital cameras" in February 2023*

The shopping-oriented results are far deeper than they were back in February 2018. In fact, there are several more screens of this type of content, showing more ecommerce sites and shopping bars.

As of June 2025, Google has released 15 core updates since March 2018. Each of these has been an effort to improve the quality of its search results. It should also be noted that Google has 25 times the market share of its largest competitors in most markets (*https://oreil.ly/DOSnp*), meaning that its ability to continuously test algorithm improvements, including the process of better understanding user intent, far eclipses that of its next closest competitor.

The reason these efforts are so important is because this type of knowledge is not native to generative AI tools. However, Google's history and dominance in search give it far more information on this than any other entity in search (or in any other realm, for that matter).

## How Government Regulation of AI Will Affect You

Governments will begin taking a larger role in regulating AI use for creating content. This can affect what you'll be able to do with AI in your organization. For example, the European Union took the first step in March 2024 when it passed the EU Artificial Intelligence Act (*https://oreil.ly/oaEZC*) (the AI Act). This included the following definitions that categorize different AI uses by level of risk:

*Unacceptable risk*
AI uses that threaten the safety, livelihood, and rights of people are generally banned with limited exceptions for use in law enforcement.

*High risk*
Uses where the potential for harm is significant but where many beneficial applications are also possible.

*Limited risk*
Applications that interact with individuals but aren't considered unacceptable or high risk.

*Minimal risk or no risk*
Any AI systems that don't belong in any of the other three categories.

The AI Act focuses on the potential for overt harm. However, we will see other types of regulations come forth as well, such as those intended to prevent plagiarism and protect the copyright of content (text, image, audio, and video). In a report (*https://oreil.ly/PR6xo*), Gartner said:

> There will also be a greater emphasis placed on watermarking and other means to authenticate high-value content. Government regulations across the globe are already holding companies accountable as they begin to require the identification of marketing content assets that AI creates. This will likely play a role in how search engines will display such digital content.

This will further aid Google in determining which content to trust the most and in preserving overall search quality.

## How Generative AI Will Affect SEO

Both Google and Bing are actively leveraging generative AI answers in their search results. You need to understand the impact this will have on SEO since it has the potential to negatively affect the clicks that Google sends to third-party websites (such as yours). In addition, some users may stop using search engines and begin to rely on generative AI tools to answer their questions directly.

There is a concern among marketers that the volume of usage of search engines will fall. Gartner (*https://oreil.ly/PR6xo*) has come out with a prediction that search engine usage will decline 25% by 2026. Given the quality issues with generative AI responses, it will be interesting to see if this prediction proves to be the case. In addition, the integration of AI responses into the traditional search results will lower clicks delivered to web sites as well. As previously mentioned, a recent study by Ahrefs showed that clicks from Google results showing AI Overviews are down by 34.5%.

For generative AI to be broadly adopted, users will either tolerate these problems or the technology must improve significantly. The challenge with the technology is that figuring out how to address its limitations is harder than it seems. In fact, in a *Wired* article (*https://oreil.ly/xEe5Q*) published in April 2023, OpenAI CEO Sam Altman suggested that the age of giant AI models was already over. Altman suggested that the logical limits of the existing technology had been reached, and simply continuing to scale it would not help the results get materially better. The *Wired* article also quotes Nick Frosst, a cofounder of Cohere (who also worked on AI at Google), on how these solutions may be made more useful:

> *"There are lots of ways of making transformers way, way better and more useful, and lots of them don't involve adding parameters to the model," he says. Frosst says that new AI model designs, or architectures, and further tuning based on human feedback are promising directions that many researchers are already exploring.*

How quickly these improvements will become available is hard to say, but the scale of investment being made is very high. For now, the current technology, with all its existing limitations, is being used to pipe generative AI responses into search engines.

## How Generative AI Will Change Search

Integration of generative AI responses into the search engine results pages (SERPs) can also affect SEO. You need to consider the impact of this because it may result in search engines sending fewer clicks to third-party websites.

### MICROSOFT COPILOT

Bing was the first search engine to integrate a generative AI solution (ChatGPT) into search, in February 2023. This was initially called Bing Chat but has since been rebranded as Copilot. You can access Copilot from the search results screen as shown in Figure 2-22.

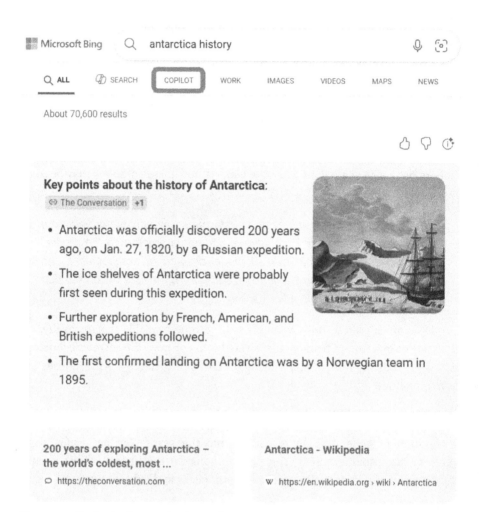

*Figure 2-22. Copilot implementation in search*

When you click the Copilot link, it renders a result like the one shown in Figure 2-23.

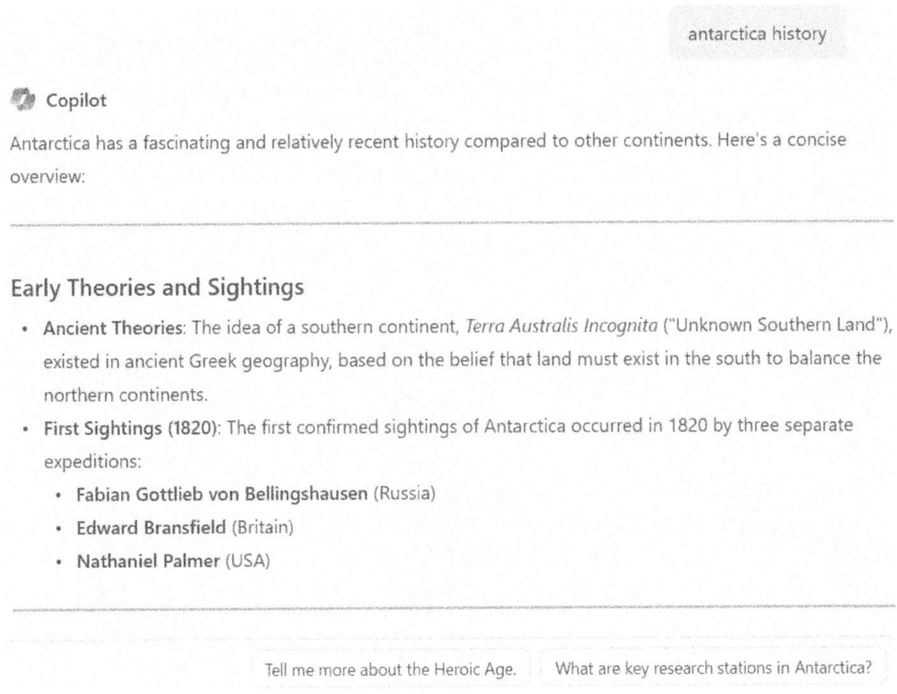

antarctica history

Copilot

Antarctica has a fascinating and relatively recent history compared to other continents. Here's a concise overview:

## Early Theories and Sightings

- **Ancient Theories**: The idea of a southern continent, *Terra Australis Incognita* ("Unknown Southern Land"), existed in ancient Greek geography, based on the belief that land must exist in the south to balance the northern continents.
- **First Sightings (1820)**: The first confirmed sightings of Antarctica occurred in 1820 by three separate expeditions:
  - **Fabian Gottlieb von Bellingshausen** (Russia)
  - **Edward Bransfield** (Britain)
  - **Nathaniel Palmer** (USA)

Tell me more about the Heroic Age.   What are key research stations in Antarctica?

*Figure 2-23. Sample Copilot result (partial result shown)*

## Note

Bing always cites sources used in its generative AI results.

There are three important characteristics of the implementation of Copilot to note:

- Copilot results are not shown on the same page as traditional search results. You must click a link to switch between search mode and chat mode.
- Copilot results are available for every query.
- Copilot always provides citations to the sources used in its results.

## GOOGLE'S AI OVERVIEWS

Google's implementation of generative AI in its SERPs in the form of AIOs (formerly called *Search Generative Experience*, or SGE) is quite different. Figure 2-24 shows a sample search query with an AIO at the top.

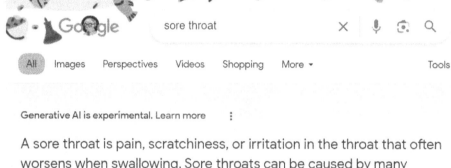

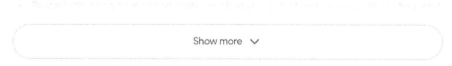

*Figure 2-24. AI overview fully integrated in Google's search results*

However, AIOs are not always integrated into the results. For example, as shown in Figure 2-25, sometimes it's made optional.

For many results, AIOs aren't even available as an option. You can see what that looks like in Figure 2-26.

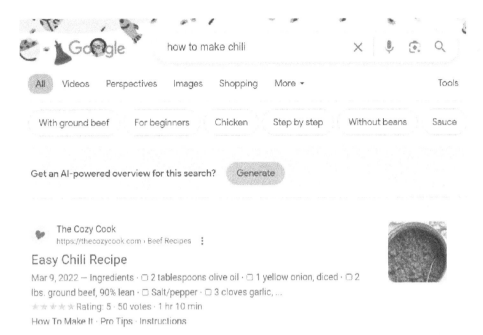

Figure 2-25. AI overview shown as an option in Google's search results

ChatGPT / Initial release date

# November 30, 2022

ChatGPT was launched on **November 30, 2022**, by San Francisco–based OpenAI (the creator of the initial GPT series of large language models; DALL. E 2, a diffusion model used to generate images; and Whisper, a speech transcription model).

Wikipedia
https://en.wikipedia.org › wiki › ChatGPT

ChatGPT - Wikipedia

Figure 2-26. Google search result with no AI Overview

In May 2025 Ahrefs released a study of 55.8 million queries (*https://oreil.ly/ xjnpK*) showing that AIOs were showing up in 12.8% of Google's search results. Another Ahrefs study showed that the AIOs had a significant impact on CTR search queries—reducing that by 34.5% to position one rankings. In addition, the integration of AI responses into the traditional search results will lower clicks delivered to web sites as well. As previously mentioned, a recent study by Ahrefs showed that clicks from Google results showing AI Overviews are down by 34.5%.

Also of note, Google introduced AI Mode in March 2025 and made it available to all US users in June 2025. AI Mode introduces a conversational chat style search option to Google Search. This is an important development, and we'll discuss the implications of it more in Chapter 8.

## Conclusion

In this chapter, we reviewed what generative AI technology is, its impact on the market, and key information about the most important generative AI tools. We also outlined the current state of generative AI technology. This included showing that it has great potential to significantly affect our capabilities, but that there are also many issues with it, which helps us understand both the power and the dangers of engaging with generative AI. Finally, we discussed how Google views AI content in search to provide further context about the best ways to use AI in our own efforts.

In the next chapter, we'll lay more groundwork for using generative AI, including understanding the key business considerations, setting the right goals, building prompting skills, and learning how to detect AI-generated content. In the chapters that follow, we'll explore the many things you can do to leverage the technology right now, including walking through numerous detailed examples.

# PART II

# Putting AI to Work

# 3

# Getting Started with Generative AI

You've seen the potential of generative AI to drive SEO growth for your organization. You've also seen plenty of problems that can arise from being too aggressive with using it. So what do you need to get started? That's what we'll address in this chapter.

Unless you want to build your own generative AI system (we cover this topic in Chapter 6), you will likely use a variety of tools to create content. This chapter focuses on both the necessary and the optional tools for optimizing content creation. Every tool has its advantages and disadvantages, so this chapter explains what can be done with these tools and the pitfalls to avoid.

For organizations that have content creation strategies, incorporating generative AI tools into those strategies requires changes to corporate procedures. Your writers, editors, and anyone else in the content-generation pipeline must learn to adjust. We'll cover some of the concerns that you and your organization might have when generative AI is integrated into your content creation process.

If you work with external contractors to help with writing, you should find out if the content they provide you was generated by AI. You're paying them for their expertise, and you want to make sure you're getting it. If AI-detection tools know that your content is machine generated, then Google can detect it as well. We cover these tools, show you how to use them, and discuss the pros and cons of using AI detection.

As you'll see throughout the chapter, there are limitations to what generative AI tools can do. Humans are required to review AI-generated content and fix any mistakes before finalizing the work. The final section of this chapter will provide examples of how you can do this.

## Learning How to Use Generative AI

There are many ways to use generative AI to help drive your SEO program. Regardless of your specific implementation, you will have to complete several high-level steps to ensure that you're applying generative AI effectively:

- Determine what tools fit your applications
- Understand key business factors
- Get your organization ready
- Set expectations for impact
- Learn how to write great prompts

We'll discuss each of these in the following sections.

### DETERMINING WHAT TOOLS BEST FIT YOUR APPLICATIONS

As you saw in Chapter 2, there are many generative AI tools you could consider using, and each has its strengths and weaknesses. Once you've decided what to use generative AI for, you'll want to pick the best tool for that application. This is an important decision as it can significantly affect the quality of the output you receive.

In Chapter 2, we explored the strengths and weaknesses of the major tools available in the market, but you must also consider how those affect the applications you have in mind. Some examples might be:

- Researching topic ideas
- Generating outlines
- Writing JSON code
- Doing math
- Summarizing content
- Brainstorming article topics
- Coming up with key data points and sources

- Analyzing content gaps
- Writing schema code
- Validating web pages
- Summarizing trends
- Updating *robots.txt* or *.htaccess* code

These are just some of the possible applications for generative AI. We'll cover these and many more in Chapters 4 and 5.

## UNDERSTANDING KEY BUSINESS FACTORS

There are many other considerations related to your business and market. Note that these factors apply to any use you may make of generative AI, not just using it for SEO. Some of these are:

*Company culture*
> Are there reasons to anticipate resistance to working with AI from either organization leaders or the broader team?

*Privacy concerns*
> How sensitive is the information you're working with? Do you prefer to avoid sharing that with any third parties, such as the provider of a generative AI tool? These types of concerns can affect how you use generative AI.

*Organizational readiness*
> How fast can your team adapt to new business processes, and how quickly can they learn to work with new technologies?

*Risk tolerance*
> Are you ready to take on the risks associated with making significant changes to how you do things? Things may not go as smoothly as you hope, and you must be prepared to work through whatever challenges arise.

*Competitive pressure*
> How aggressively are your competitors embracing AI? Are some of them already gaining a competitive advantage with it? This type of pressure can force you to get more aggressive than you might otherwise be inclined to do.

*Granularity of your topic*
> If your organization works on the bleeding edge of research in a highly technical area, there may not be much written material on the web about that area. This may limit how much you can expect generative AI tools to be able to help you.

*International concerns*
> Some countries have legislation governing generative AI. For example, the European Union AI Act (*https://oreil.ly/q_wlk*) governs the use of AI for social scoring and government use of the technology.

## GETTING YOUR ORGANIZATION READY

Change can be challenging in many ways. In the case of AI, several of your staff members may be concerned about changes to their job security or the impact on future employment. It's important for organizations to start by educating staff on the ways that generative AI can speed up their job functions and make them more productive. Employees may also be concerned about learning a new and unfamiliar technology. Education is the key here, and there are many ways to provide that:

*Announce company initiatives in AI*

Be open about what you're doing and why you're doing it. Communicate this with excitement about how it can help the company grow and the opportunities it will create.

*Promote AI at company meetings*

Hold one or more special meetings to discuss plans for using AI or add a discussion about it to broader company meetings (such as quarterly or annual updates).

*Hold AI-specific training sessions*

Announce and hold meetings to train staff on how to use AI. These can be company-wide or one department at a time. Trainings can help people become comfortable with the strengths and weaknesses of AI as well as help them understand how to apply AI in their jobs.

*Use "lunch and learns" to promote AI*

These serve a similar purpose as the AI-specific training sessions but are meant to be supplemental. You can make them optional and use them to learn which of your employees are most interested in the topic.

*Provide access to tools*

The more your employees become familiar with using generative AI tools, the better. Grant them access with appropriate training so that they have that opportunity. Require them to sign up so that you can get further indication of who has the most interest in becoming AI literate.

*Address concerns*

Provide team members with a way to ask questions and express concerns. Respond to these actively to help maximize the engagement of your team with generative AI.

Just as with the key business factors in the previous section, this list applies to any use you may make of generative AI, not just SEO.

## SETTING EXPECTATIONS FOR IMPACT

In "Limitations of Generative AI" on page 53, we discussed many aspects of the shortcomings of generative AI tools. These issues mean that we can't use the output of the tools without including expert human review. If you don't incorporate this human review, you're taking on a high risk with every output you apply from the tools within your business.

Therefore, you can't hand generative AI the keys to the bus and expect everything to come out well. You need to involve expert humans in reviewing all outputs. The key is to make sure that humans own the results of the work, regardless of how you use the tools.

This limits the scope of the impact. For example, if you're using generative AI to help you create content, here are some example expectations you might have:

- Cut content creation costs by 30%

- Increase throughput by 30%

- Improve quality by 20%

The truth is that these results are pretty spectacular. If content creation is a large part of what your organization does, it would be a game changer for you. Note that your results may differ from these, but they do represent reasonable targets.

To illustrate further, here are some great activities that you could use generative AI to help you with:

*Check the code of a web page for SEO problems*
> This is valuable if you understand its limitations. It may not catch all errors ("missed issues"), and it may report some things as errors that aren't problems ("false positives"). *False positives* are alerts for errors that aren't actually errors. You want true positives, which means your generative AI prompts correctly identify errors on the page. If you've written a good prompt, the missed issues and false positives will still happen from time to time, but the actual errors found ("true positives") will be invaluable to you, and the missed issues and false positives are easily identified with human review. We discuss this use case more in Chapter 5.

*Write schema code*

> This provides the developer with a draft of code to review and finalize. It's better than starting with a blank sheet of paper! We also discuss this use case more in Chapter 5.

*Write content*

> You can also use generative AI to assist with writing content because it can provide the writer with something to start with other than a blank sheet of paper. This can involve drafting outlines, paragraphs, and articles. This is a complicated topic with many layers, and we cover it in detail in Chapter 4.

## LEARNING HOW TO WRITE GREAT PROMPTS

Success in working with generative AI depends on the quality of the prompts you write, so you must learn how to write great prompts to maximize your results. We'll discuss the basics of prompt writing in this section. This is not meant to be a comprehensive guide but should provide a strong starting place.

### Must-Dos

Here are the critical elements of effective prompting:

*Identify your target audience*

> Your prompt should provide this information so that the generative AI tools can tune their responses accordingly. Just a few examples of target audiences are second-grade students, buyers of equipment for industrial kitchens, developers looking for sample source code, parents of newborn children, and nuclear physicists. You can be extremely specific or more general, depending on the nature of what you're trying to do.

*Establish your persona*

> This is similar to your brand voice. Do you want to sound authoritative, academic, lighthearted, friendly? The tools are generally good at adapting to these types of instructions. An example might be: "You are a manufacturer of lawn tractors for industrial use, and the content you write should be authoritative in tone but easy to read."

*Provide context*

> Provide your generative AI tool with additional info about your target audience. For example, if you're targeting parents of newborn children, are they looking for advice? Or something to buy to fill a need? Let the AI know what your target audience wants to see.

## Dos and don'ts

Clearly detail in your prompt what you want the generative AI to do and what you don't want it to do. For example: "Give me a biography of Winston Churchill, but don't give me information about his childhood." Figure 3-1 shows this prompt and a portion of the response received from Gemini.

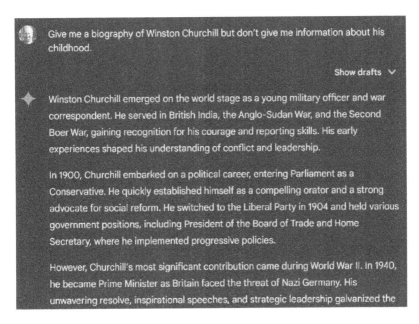

*Figure 3-1. Gemini's response to a prompt*

## Progressively iterate your prompts

Make your initial prompt as high quality as possible but know that generative AI tools treat conversations with you like chat sessions. That means that once you get a response to your initial prompt, you can provide input on how you would like to tweak it. For example, perhaps you asked for a bio of Danny Sullivan and got a bio for Danny Sullivan the search expert, which wasn't what you wanted. If so, you can try something like "Please update your response to focus on Danny Sullivan the race car driver." You can see this illustrated in the figures in the following section, "An Example of Iterative Prompting" on page 91. The tool will then give you an updated response. You can also make simpler iterations, such as "Please don't use so many superlatives in your response."

*Describe your preferred output format*

Do you want something written as an article? A bulleted list? A spreadsheet? Source code? A haiku? Be specific about this to get the formatting you're looking for.

*Use the special features of the tool*

Each of the major generative AI tools has its special features. These features may address specific needs that you have for your project. For example, as of this writing, ChatGPT is beta testing features for automation that enable you to have it execute tasks on a specific schedule. For example, you can use this feature to summarize the latest AI news on a daily basis for you. Which features each tool has will change, so it makes sense to keep checking feature updates of each tool to find the one that best fits the needs of your particular projects.

## Gotchas

The aforementioned elements of an effective prompt will provide a good start, but you also should avoid common errors. Some of these are:

*Vagueness*

If your prompt is vague, chances are good that the response will not be what you want. An example here might be "Tell me about life on Earth." Instead, try something more specific, such as "Please tell me about the evolution of the early hominids" or "How did the first single-celled organisms come into existence on Earth?"

*Over-specification*

If you are too prescriptive, it may also be difficult for the tool to understand how to meet your needs.

*Providing too much information*

If you provide a lot of detailed information in your prompt, it can be hard for the tool to understand what is most important or what to include and omit.

*Failure to provide context*

Providing the tool with a clear context is important. If you're unclear, you'll likely run into problems. For example, you ask, "What's the best time to fly to Singapore?" This leaves us with many questions, such as:

- From where?

- For what purpose? Business? Vacation?

- Is the question about the time of day, day of the week, or time of year?

- A better way to ask might be "What is the best time to fly to Singapore from New York for a holiday during winter in New York?"

*Figurative language*

Figurative language can include metaphors, hyperbole, allusion, similes, and more. An example is "She's as smart as a whip." Your generative AI tool will have trouble following along!

Learning how to create great prompts takes practice, so allow some time for your team to practice and get good at doing it before you assign them to a critical project. Chances are that the knowledge of how to do this will be prevalent by the end of 2026, but for now, plan on a learning curve to develop this expertise. If someone works hard at this and experiments a lot, they can probably become pretty good within two to three months and have a high level of expertise within a year.

## An Example of Iterative Prompting

As we discussed previously, your first attempt with a prompt may not give you the results you're looking for. That's OK, though, as most generative AI tools are designed to be interactive. This means you can review the output you receive and then ask the tool to modify it. Let's start with an example, shown in Figure 3-2, where we ask Claude 3 Opus, "Who is Danny Sullivan?"

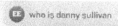
who is danny sullivan

Danny Sullivan is a technologist, journalist, and widely recognized expert in the field of search engine optimization (SEO). Some key points about him:

1. Sullivan started covering search engines in 1995 and has been a leading voice in the industry ever since. He founded Search Engine Watch, one of the earliest and most influential publications about search engines, in 1997.

2. In 2006, he co-founded Search Engine Land, another highly respected publication in the search industry, and served as its Chief Content Officer for over a decade.

3. Sullivan has been a frequent speaker at search engine and digital marketing conferences worldwide, educating businesses and professionals about SEO best practices and trends.

4. In 2017, Sullivan joined Google as their Public Liaison for Search, serving as the company's public face for communication about search-related issues. His role involves explaining how Google search works and engaging with the search community.

5. Sullivan has been instrumental in pushing for greater transparency from search engines about how they rank content and in helping to establish industry standards and best practices for SEO.

Throughout his career, Danny Sullivan has been a key figure in helping people understand the complex and ever-evolving world of search engines and online marketing.

*Figure 3-2. Initial response to the question "Who is Danny Sullivan?" by Claude 3 Opus*

This looks like a pretty solid response, but unfortunately, we wanted the information to be about the famous race car driver, so let's try telling Claude that and ask it to try again, as shown in Figure 3-3.

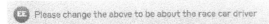

Danny Sullivan is a retired American race car driver who had a successful career in open-wheel racing. Some key points about him:

1. Sullivan began his racing career in the 1970s, competing in various Formula Ford series in the United States and Europe.

2. In 1982, he made his debut in the Indianapolis 500, where he would go on to compete 12 times. His best finish at the Indy 500 was a win in 1985.

3. Sullivan won the CART (Championship Auto Racing Teams) championship in 1988, driving for Penske Racing. He achieved 17 race wins and 19 pole positions in his CART career.

4. One of Sullivan's most famous moments in racing came during the 1985 Indianapolis 500 when he lost control of his car, spun 360 degrees, and miraculously recovered to continue the race. He went on to win the race, and the moment became known as the "Spin and Win."

5. After retiring from full-time racing in 1995, Sullivan worked as a commentator and analyst for ABC and ESPN's coverage of open-wheel racing.

Throughout his career, Danny Sullivan was known for his smooth driving style, consistency, and ability to perform well under pressure. He was inducted into the Motorsports Hall of Fame of America in 2012, cementing his status as one of the most successful American open-wheel racers of his generation.

*Figure 3-3. Response to the question "Who is Danny Sullivan the race car driver?" by Claude 3 Opus*

This is great, but our intended audience is 10-year-old children, so we'd like to adjust this more. Let's try that with another request to Claude 3 Opus to tweak the output, shown in Figure 3-4.

> **EE** This is great but please change target the content to 10 year old children

Hey there, kids! Let me tell you about a really cool race car driver named Danny Sullivan!

1. Danny started racing cars when he was young, just like you! He loved going super fast and competing against other racers.

2. He got to race in a big event called the Indianapolis 500 a whole bunch of times. That's like the Super Bowl of car racing! In 1985, he even won the race!

3. In 1988, Danny became the champion of a racing group called CART. That means he was the best driver in the whole group that year!

4. One time during a race in 1985, something really crazy happened. Danny's car started spinning around in circles, but he was so good at driving that he was able to get the car going straight again and keep racing. It was like a real-life superhero moment!

5. After he stopped racing, Danny talked about racing on TV. He got to share all the cool things he learned about cars and racing with people watching at home.

Danny Sullivan was an amazing race car driver who loved going fast and had some incredible moments on the racetrack. He showed that with hard work and determination, you can achieve your dreams, just like he did!

Copy  Retry

*Figure 3-4. Response to "Who is Danny Sullivan?" modified for 10-year-olds*

This looks pretty good, but it's a bit long, so let's ask Claude to shorten the response. You can see the results in Figure 3-5.

> **EE** Please shorten your response to 3 paragraphs

Hey there, kids! Let me tell you about a really cool race car driver named Danny Sullivan!

Danny was born in a place called Louisville, and he loved racing cars ever since he was a little kid, just like you! He started racing when he was a grown-up and became really good at it. He even got to race in super special kinds of race cars called Formula One cars and IndyCars, which are incredibly fast and hard to drive!

In 1985, Danny won the most famous IndyCar race of all - the Indianapolis 500! During the race, his car spun around in a complete circle, but he was such a good driver that he was able to keep going and win the race anyway. Isn't that amazing? He kept racing IndyCars for many years, winning lots more races and even becoming the champion of all the IndyCar drivers in 1988! After he stopped racing, Danny became a TV star and talked about racing so that everyone could learn more about it. He's now remembered as one of the greatest race car drivers ever!

*Figure 3-5. Response to "Who is Danny Sullivan?" shortened to three paragraphs*

As you can see, Claude 3 Opus complied with our request, but the response wasn't quite what we expected since the third paragraph is quite long. It did what we asked but didn't meet our intent, so let's try one more tweak, shown in Figure 3-6.

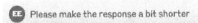

Hey kids, let me tell you about a really cool race car driver named Danny Sullivan!

Danny loved racing cars ever since he was a little kid, just like you! He raced in super fast cars called Formula One and IndyCars. In 1985, he even won the famous Indianapolis 500 race after spinning around in a complete circle and still managing to keep going. How amazing is that?

Danny won lots more races and became the champion of all IndyCar drivers in 1988. He's now remembered as one of the greatest race car drivers ever! So, if you dream of being a race car driver someday, just remember Danny Sullivan and never give up on your dreams!

*Figure 3-6. Response to "Who is Danny Sullivan?" shortened even more*

You can keep tweaking the output until you get something very close to what you want. This process is helpful for people who are just learning how to prompt as it can show you how to write better initial prompts. As your prompting improves, notice that the output conveys your message much more accurately, including the right tone and style for your brand. Compare the generative AI responses before and after to identify improvements and to build a strategy behind generating the output that you want.

In the case of our example, we could have specified that we wanted the race car driver and to target an audience of 10-year-old children up front. However, even experts at prompting should expect to do some of this iterative prompting.

## Detecting AI-Generated Content

Another area where you need to develop your team's skills is in detecting AI-generated content. This is important for two reasons:

*Because Google will*
As discussed in Chapter 2, Google is very concerned that poor-quality content written by AI will flood the web. You can use generative AI to assist in creating content, but the content must show expertise, experi-

ence, authoritativeness, and trustworthiness (*https://oreil.ly/F1VPo*). Google is actively working to detect AI-generated content to prevent it from ranking and polluting the quality of its search results. This means that the content you generate with AI may significantly damage your site's ranking potential.

*Your writers may be misusing it*

If you are paying external writers to create original content, you need to ensure that they are not providing you with poorly edited—or even unedited—AI-generated content. If they are, that could also harm your site's SEO potential. As previously discussed, publishing poor-quality, AI-generated content could lead to a loss of authoritative signals sent to Google's algorithms. Misuse of AI is also unethical because the dishonest writers are passing off AI-generated work as their own with the intention of receiving full compensation for it.

Therefore, it's critical to have processes to run all content you create for your site through AI detection before you publish it.

Building your team's skills in AI detection will require some investment on your part. There is no simple, guaranteed way to do this. You'll need to make use of third-party tools to help you identify content that *may* be written by AI, and then your editors will need to review the content to check it for quality.

## AI-DETECTION TOOLS

There are many tools for detecting AI-written content. Some of the more well-known ones, as of this writing, include:

- AI Text Classifier (*https://oreil.ly/9I3uv*)
- BrandWell (formerly Content-AtScale) (*https://oreil.ly/upyvv*)
- Copyleaks (*https://oreil.ly/6DoPK*)
- Crossplag (*https://crossplag.com*)
- GLTR (*http://gltr.io*)
- GPTZero (*https://gptzero.me*)
- Originality.AI (*https://oreil.ly/xaiv8*)
- Sapling (*https://oreil.ly/fuRoT*)
- Undetectable (*https://undetectable.ai*)
- Winston AI (*https://gowinston.ai*)
- Writer (*https://oreil.ly/uz_l7*)
- ZeroGPT (*https://oreil.ly/wJqDk*)

These tools are constantly evolving. Before you choose one or more of them to use in your organization, read the latest third-party reviews to see which one might work best for you. You can also see what influencers you respect are suggesting.

## HOW AI DETECTION WORKS

In Chapter 2, we discussed the limitations of the generative AI tools. Based on those, there are many major criteria that AI-detection tools look for. Some of these include:

*Overt errors in the content*
> You can see examples in Figures 2-11 and 2-12. The errors in Figure 2-11 might be harder for an AI detection tool to catch because this is also incorrect in many human-written articles on the web. However, Figure 2-12 shows a more obvious error where you can't find any human-written content on the web with that same mistake.

*Odd word choices*
> Generative AI tools are known for making unusual word choices when they create content. Sometimes the text comes through with an unusual number of adjectives and/or adverbs in it, or words get reused many different times in a block of text. A quick human review of the text will leave the reviewer feeling that the writing style is a bit odd.

*Lack of variations in sentence length*
> AI-written content tends to have more consistent sentence length than human-written content. This is referred to as "burstiness."

*Unnecessary duplication of content*
> AI-written content tends to repeat key points in a way that is not needed. You can see an example of this in Figure 2-6.

The tools aren't perfect at detecting problems, but they will catch a decent percentage of content that has been written by AI. Be aware, however, that Google likely has a much more sophisticated process for detecting AI than the commercial tools provide.

## What Makes Content Valuable

It's important to take a moment to consider what makes content useful to users because this is the content that Google's algorithms are designed to detect and rank. Understanding this can help you decide how best to use generative AI to assist in creating that type of content.

### Note

Google's algorithms are by no means perfect, so there are times when they fail to rank the best content and may even rank poor-quality content. Nonetheless, Google works continuously to improve these algorithms, so it's best to target making your content the best content.

Consider the search example shown in Figure 3-7. The query is "how to make French toast," including the quotation marks around the text. Quotes around the text forces Google to return only pages with that exact string.

*Figure 3-7. Forcing Google to return pages with an exact string*

Note that on the right side of the image, Google says that it has "about 85,000 results" for this query. That's a lot of pages discussing how to make French toast! With that in mind, if you choose to create another page on this topic, what do you think the chances are that you'll be bringing some new value about it to the web? The chances are slim.

The reason for sharing this example is that it relates to what you get with AI-generated content. Since this content is a regeneration of things that the AI tool has seen on the internet, it can't bring anything new to anyone. It's all old information. Given this context, Google has little incentive to rank it in their search results.

So what content does Google think is valuable? Google has provided some insight by publishing their Search Quality Rater Guidelines (SQRGs) (*https://oreil.ly/XVt1T*). These are guidelines that Google provides to people who manually evaluate the quality of Google's search results ("Quality Raters"). These Quality Raters review Google's search results, examine pages that earn high-ranking positions, and then score those pages. Based on these scores, Google can see how well its algorithms are doing at providing quality content in the results.

We can use these guidelines to help us understand what content is high quality. Within these guidelines, Google exposes us to other concepts related to content quality. One of these is EEAT. These are metrics for evaluating the likelihood that the publishing site and author are good resources for the information they are providing. Based on Google's guidelines, here is what each of the letters in EEAT means:

*Experience*
> Does the writer have firsthand or life experience with the topic? Of course, generative AI tools have no firsthand experience; all they do is spin off text based on what they have already seen published on the internet.

*Expertise*
> Does the writer have the knowledge or skill to create quality content on the topic?

*Authoritativeness*
> Do others in the market see the writer as an authority on the topic?

*Trust*
> The SQRGs note that this is the most important of the EEAT signals because untrustworthy pages shouldn't rank even if they score well on experience, expertise, and authoritativeness.

Now let's discuss how EEAT would be viewed for AI-generated content:

*Experience*
> The AI has no real-world experience, so score this one as a zero.

*Expertise*
> The AI has no expertise either. The "knowledge" you see within generative AI responses is simply scraped from the web and regurgitated in a rewritten manner. The score for this metric would also be zero.

*Authoritativeness*
> While many people are currently excited about how "smart" the tools are, this will likely fade as people get tired of all the errors, omissions, and other problems. Except in certain specific situations, Google will score this

very low, too. In addition, if you're using AI to be your "authority" on something, your actual authoritativeness in the market will erode.

*Trust*

It's difficult to assess how much "trust" Google would put in an AI algorithm unless there is a specific reason to do so.

## Note

As a reminder, in Chapter 1 we noted that EEAT isn't a direct ranking factor, except for sites focused on health or financial topics, but the role of the Quality Raters is to indicate how they think content should be ranked, and they are expected to consider EEAT and many other factors related to content quality for all sites. The Google algorithm then uses other ranking signals to attempt to rank the best content first.

Not all AI-generated content is considered bad. There are examples of areas where Google has trusted AI-created content for quite some time. A couple of examples are weather-related and earnings report queries. Figure 3-8 shows an example query for "Wells Fargo earnings report."

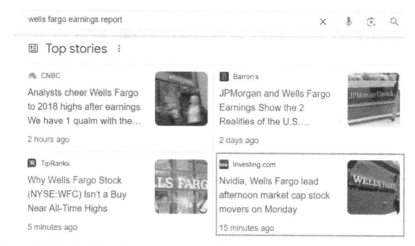

*Figure 3-8. Wells Fargo earnings report query result in Google*

The information in the highlighted result is AI generated. Yet Google trusts this information because it's a simple presentation of the data, and Investing.com has very high scores from an authoritativeness perspective.

Another example is a sports play-by-play. If you have a favorite team that is playing while you're out to dinner, you might pick up your phone and enter a quick query, such as "49ers play-by-play." You'll get a response back that is also AI generated.

From Google's perspective, these types of situations are OK because:

- The content created was highly constrained by the data input into the algorithm.
- The publishers of the content that Google chooses to rank in the search results have a demonstrated history of authoritativeness and trust.

Ultimately, the idea of having AI create content isn't a fundamental problem for Google. Poor-quality content is a problem for Google, and this is regardless of whether AI was involved in creating it or not. However, as we've discussed in Chapter 2 and this chapter, when AI is used to create content, it's prone to making mistakes, and since it only regurgitates what is already on the internet, it doesn't provide new insights. These are issues for Google.

With these things in mind, let's now summarize the key things that Google is looking for in content:

- Content that is unique and answers questions that other content on the web doesn't
- Content that focuses on adding value to users

### Note

What "adding value" means depends heavily on user queries. Some users may be looking to buy something right now; in other cases, the user only wants information.

The E, E, and A parts of EEAT relate to these two concepts. As for trust, you can think of this as being strongly correlated with brand. A strong brand is something that many larger companies have, but individuals who are experts in their field can also have a strong brand. Users tend to associate a strong brand with credibility and trustworthiness. For that reason, it's important to build a strong brand in your market—for your company, for your key SMEs, or for both.

In summary, Google wants your content to add value to users. Re-creating content that already exists on the web, that has errors or omissions, or that doesn't focus on providing value to users isn't what Google is looking to rank on its search engine. If you choose to use generative AI to assist you in creating content, make sure that you address these concerns. We'll talk about one of the most important components of doing that in the next section.

## Requiring Human Involvement

In Chapter 2 and this chapter, we have emphasized the need for deliberate human involvement whenever an AI tool is used. Although generative AI tools are very powerful, they are still prone to making mistakes that can only be caught by humans. You need to plan for SMEs on your team to review and finalize any and all AI-generated work. As a reminder, some of the issues to be concerned about include:

*Errors*
> These are cases where generative AI provides false information.

*Omissions*
> These are responses that forget to include important information.

*Context misalignment*
> Even after you carefully craft your prompt and include the context that you are looking for, the generative AI tool may still get it wrong.

*Not fitting your brand voice*
> Even if you provide brand-voice instructions in your prompts, the generative AI tool may still make mistakes with it.

Ultimately, your workflow should require human involvement to review and finalize the work. Here are some examples to illustrate how this should work:

- If you use AI to audit the SEO of a web page, have an experienced technical SEO professional review the findings for accuracy. Also have them check the web page for issues that the AI might have missed. These errors can range from not understanding the context of the code to failing to parse the code correctly, leading to false positives or missing issues completely.

- If you use AI to write JSON code to support schema on a web page, have an experienced JSON programmer who understands schema coding check the code for accuracy before publishing it.

- If you use AI to generate an outline for an article you plan to write, have an SME review and update the outline before starting to write it. Better still, have the generative AI tool create three outlines and then have the SME fact-check and merge them into a more in-depth outline before starting to write the article.

These examples are only meant to illustrate the broader concept: you need to include humans in your content review, ideally in the form of an SME who will be responsible for the quality of the published content. This will require them to fact-check the output, correct errors, identify significant omissions, and remove content that doesn't belong.

## Conclusion

In this chapter, we've tried to cover everything you need to consider at a high level before you can begin applying generative AI within your organization. In the next chapter, we'll discuss how you can use generative AI to help you create content, and in Chapter 5, we'll discuss how you can use generative AI to help you with your SEO tasks.

# 4

# Using AI to Scale Content Development

If you can work around the limitations, generative AI can bring substantial leverage to your content development efforts. The key is to learn how to include SME reviews at critical points during your content creation process.

### Note

This philosophy will also serve you well in creating content for ranking in LLM tools such as ChatGPT, Copilot, Gemini, and Claude.

As a simple example, consider the process of drafting an outline for a new piece of content. Without AI, writing content from scratch is hard. The writer starts with a blank page, and it's up to them to figure out what the piece should be about, what topics it should cover, and in what order. Even if an experienced SME is involved to help verify accuracy and relevance, there's a chance that the writer may have overlooked all the topics that should be addressed in the new content.

With AI, it's a different story. Think of generative AI as a brainstorming partner for non-SME writers that helps them come up with a broad range of topic ideas. It can surface relevant ideas for a new piece of content that the writer or even an SME may not have thought of. Even if the generative AI tool's suggestions aren't a great fit or are outright wrong, an SME should be able to recognize easily which ones are relevant or could be corrected. This will give writers a great start at completing the task in front of them, which offers significant benefits to the throughput of content creation and can improve content quality at the same time.

In this chapter, we'll talk about the importance of involving SMEs throughout your content development process. We'll show you numerous ways to use AI to improve your content creation, including using it to:

- Research topics
- Generate outlines
- Draft titles
- Draft meta descriptions
- Identify content gaps
- Generate database-driven content

- Generate FAQs
- Source data and statistics
- Create a list of relevant questions
- Summarize content
- Create a list of trends

This is by no means a complete list of the ways you can use AI to improve your content development process. At the end of the chapter, we'll address how you can bring it all together to maximize how you leverage AI in helping your writing team create content.

## Set Reasonable Goals for Impact

In "Setting Expectations for Impact" on page 87, we discussed setting appropriate goals for how much you can expect to gain from your use of generative AI. When you are considering projects designed to cut costs, increase speed (throughput), and improve quality, normally you'll find that you can achieve only two of these three goals in any one project. This limitation is real, unless you are applying a disruptive new technology.

Generative AI *is* a disruptive technology, so you can potentially target cutting the costs of creating content, increasing throughput, and improving quality all at the same time. But temper your expectations a bit. You shouldn't set a goal of reducing costs by 50% and increasing throughput by 100%—it's just not realistic. Consider more modest goals, such as cutting costs by 20%–30%, increasing throughput by 20%–30%, and improving quality by 20%. These more modest goals are more realistic. Keep that in mind as you go through this chapter.

## The Role of Subject Matter Experts

In "What You Need to Know About What Google Wants" on page 14, we discussed the type of content that Google wants to include in its search results. That discussion included these key points:

- The subject matter expertise of the author
- The author's level of direct experience with the content
- Whether your site is considered authoritative on the topic
- If users trust your organization and website in your chosen subject area
- Whether your content brings unique new expertise or perspectives on the topic

While Google isn't perfect at detecting these aspects of your content, that is what it strives to do, and it keeps getting better at it. If you fail to address these factors, you run the risk of your content not ranking well and wasting the investment you made.

We've also previously discussed that generative AI can't address these factors well. Neither can a writer who isn't an SME. This is important to internalize if you are in charge of putting together or managing a content development team. An SME must have final ownership of all content you create to ensure that the content they are involved with is of very high quality. The SME could be a power user of your product or someone who can write content about your industry from an authoritative perspective—not a writer who cannot verify the accuracy or relevance of material or come up with insightful content.

## Tip

One way to help motivate SMEs is to put their name on the article (as an author or an editor). A byline from an SME also provides an authoritative element and might stimulate more trust from readers.

If you fail to have an SME play a key role in your AI-supported content development process, you risk republishing thoughts and ideas that have been shared by many others before. It won't stand out. Worse, some of the information in the content may be off topic or inaccurate, or you may fail to include some key points that you should be making.

For that reason, SMEs are critical to your content development process, and you'll see many references to them throughout this chapter and the rest of this book as part of your overall AI-supported SEO strategy. The role of a non-SME writer (or simply, a "writer") is to draft content. Generative AI tools support an SME creating content as well, albeit in a different way. The SME's role in content generation is to ensure that the content is authoritative and does not have errors, especially errors by omission.

## Using Generative AI to Help with Content Creation and Editing

With these modest goals in mind, let's review specific ways you can leverage generative AI in your content development process.

### RESEARCHING TOPICS

Coming up with article ideas can be challenging, but this is one of the many ways generative AI can help. Many organizations begin this process by performing keyword research, and this is useful input to the process of coming up with topics for articles on your site. Hopefully, you're already supplementing your keyword research with ideas generated by your writers and SMEs.

Topic generation is one thing that generative AI tools can do extremely well. They can come up with fresh ideas that neither your keyword research nor your SMEs will surface. This is potentially of huge value to your SEO program. The key insight is that keyword research tools don't show all the search terms users might use when searching for something. The reason they don't is simple: they only sample a small percentage of the traffic on the web and miss most of the long-tail search terms that users enter related to your seed term. However, generative AI tools use a different dataset and may make different suggestions than you would see in traditional keyword research tools. This fits nicely into how Google's algorithms work since Google wants to send traffic to sites that provide the most value to users, and covering long-tail topics is part of what you need to satisfy a large percentage of your visitors.

Many people believe that addressing long-tail concerns is a waste of time and budget. They may think that the search volume is too low or that the expense of creating such content is too high. But consider the data from Ahrefs (*https://oreil.ly/BRWC_*) that shows that 95% of all keywords are long tail, representing 35% of all search volume. That's a lot of opportunity to leave on the table, especially since long-tail keywords tend to be more specific and therefore can have higher conversions than other search queries.

Another factor to consider is that data from the Google leak of May 27, 2024 (*https://oreil.ly/oGoa8*), shows that Google monitors user behavior on websites in great detail. We can infer from this that Google considers the total user experience on your site and that SEO isn't judged on a simple page-by-page basis. In other words, broad coverage of long-tail topics on other pages on your site can help your main pages rank for the head terms they target.

Therefore, using many approaches to researching topic areas is very important to your overall strategy.

Figure 4-1 shows a portion of the response from ChatGPT-4o to the prompt "Suggest some article topics related to someone considering a personal loan." Note that how you write your prompts is critical to the quality of the outputs that you get back from your generative AI tool of choice. We share simple examples of prompts throughout this chapter (and Chapter 5), but investing time in crafting great prompts is worthwhile.

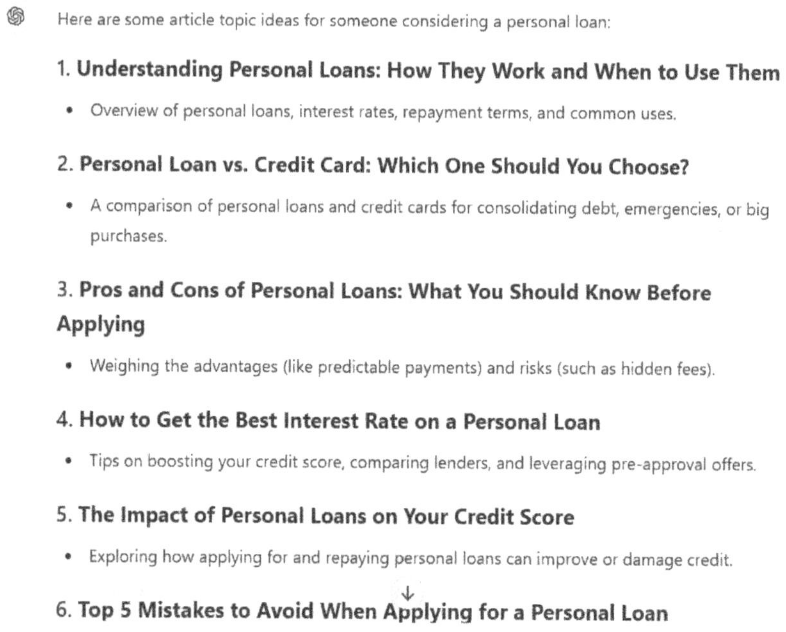

Here are some article topic ideas for someone considering a personal loan:

**1. Understanding Personal Loans: How They Work and When to Use Them**

- Overview of personal loans, interest rates, repayment terms, and common uses.

**2. Personal Loan vs. Credit Card: Which One Should You Choose?**

- A comparison of personal loans and credit cards for consolidating debt, emergencies, or big purchases.

**3. Pros and Cons of Personal Loans: What You Should Know Before Applying**

- Weighing the advantages (like predictable payments) and risks (such as hidden fees).

**4. How to Get the Best Interest Rate on a Personal Loan**

- Tips on boosting your credit score, comparing lenders, and leveraging pre-approval offers.

**5. The Impact of Personal Loans on Your Credit Score**

- Exploring how applying for and repaying personal loans can improve or damage credit.

**6. Top 5 Mistakes to Avoid When Applying for a Personal Loan**

*Figure 4-1. Example of ChatGPT-4o topic suggestions*

Fifteen topics were suggested in the response. You can take this further by requesting more ideas specific to each subtopic. For example, you can try a follow-on query, such as "Can you provide more detailed ideas related to the top five mistakes to avoid when applying for a personal loan?" Figure 4-2 shows the start of the response received from ChatGPT-4o to this query.

You can keep iterating in this manner until you have detailed outlines for subcategories identified in the starting list of topic ideas. There are several ways to iterate on the first article list provided (as shown in Figure 4-2):

- Introduce new subtopics
- Expand on subtopics provided in the initial response
- Continue to request more detailed descriptions

### 1. Not Shopping Around for the Best Rates and Terms

- **Problem:** Many borrowers apply with the first lender they encounter, missing out on better offers.

- Solution:

  - Compare rates from multiple lenders, including banks, credit unions, and online lenders.

  - Look for pre-qualification options with soft credit checks to see potential offers without hurting your credit.

  - Highlight how small differences in interest rates (e.g., 1-2%) can significantly affect long-term repayment costs.

### 2. Borrowing More Than You Need or Can Afford

- **Problem:** Borrowers sometimes apply for higher loan amounts because they qualify, leading to unnecessary debt.

- Solution:

  - Explain the risks of taking on more debt than necessary.

*Figure 4-2. More detailed topic suggestions from ChatGPT-4o*

Another way to enhance this process is to include a list of the existing content you have on the topic in the problem you give to your chosen generative AI tool. Keep in mind that you're using generative AI tools as brainstorming partners to generate ideas that your writers and SMEs can then run with. The core value to using generative AI is enabling your writers and SMEs to produce content more quickly and cover your topics more deeply.

## GENERATING OUTLINES

AI tools can create draft article outlines for the writer to consider using. These can give writers a starting place and reduce the chances that they will forget important subtopics.

Of course, generative AI is prone to making mistakes. One way to help address this is to ask the AI to create three different outlines for each article. The SME can then merge these into a single outline. Alternatively, you can use a reasoning model such as ChatGPT-4 to review the three outlines and combine them into one draft for you. You can also ask it to explain why it chose to combine the outlines in the way that it did. (Why did it choose the items that it did? Why did it leave some aspect out?)

Each of the outlines will likely surface some different aspects of the topic, and merging these can help minimize the chances of gaps in the final outline. In addition, your SME can ensure that the AI tool doesn't introduce overt errors into the outline.

Figure 4-3 shows a portion of a response from Gemini to the prompt "Generate an article outline on how to make French toast."

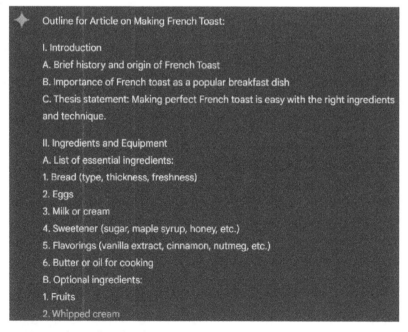

*Figure 4-3. Sample article outline from Gemini*

As you can see, the response is quite lengthy, and the screenshot shared here shows only the equipment needed, the basic ingredients, and part of the optional ingredients. Perhaps the total response is longer than we want, so let's ask Gemini to give us a shorter version. In the same session, we'll try a revised prompt: "Please shorten the outline to 10 easy steps." You can see the response in Figure 4-4.

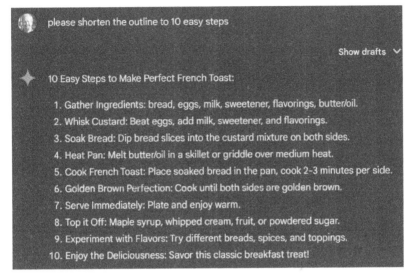

Figure 4-4. *Simpler article outline by Gemini*

We may be happy with this outline but want to add an introduction targeting new cooking students. Figure 4-5 shows what happens when we ask Gemini to do that.

You can keep going through these kinds of iterations until you get the type of article outline that you're looking for. In the process, you'll learn what you want to include in your initial prompts for future outlines, which may reduce the number of steps you need to take.

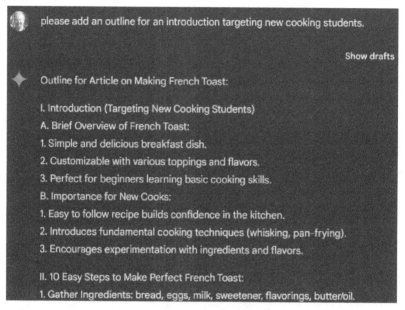

please add an outline for an introduction targeting new cooking students.

Show drafts

Outline for Article on Making French Toast:

I. Introduction (Targeting New Cooking Students)
A. Brief Overview of French Toast:
1. Simple and delicious breakfast dish.
2. Customizable with various toppings and flavors.
3. Perfect for beginners learning basic cooking skills.
B. Importance for New Cooks:
1. Easy to follow recipe builds confidence in the kitchen.
2. Introduces fundamental cooking techniques (whisking, pan-frying).
3. Encourages experimentation with ingredients and flavors.

II. 10 Easy Steps to Make Perfect French Toast:
1. Gather Ingredients: bread, eggs, milk, sweetener, flavorings, butter/oil.

*Figure 4-5. Simpler article outline with an introduction by Gemini*

## DRAFTING TITLES

You may have a web page that you've already published for which you want to consider a different title tag. Perhaps the current one isn't fully on target or isn't providing good organic search traffic, so you want to try something else. Generative AI tools are great at suggesting many different title tags for a page. Bear in mind that generative AI tools don't offer any insight into keyword search volumes, but the lack of keyword search volume is arguably a good thing.

It's great to get data that includes search volumes, and you should use it. However, it's not ideal to consider only one source of information for a title tag, and a perspective that doesn't include search volumes may open new avenues of thought for you. You can take suggestions from your LLM of choice, but you should also take your own expertise and the subject matter into consideration. Some SEO professionals also consider their competitor analysis and gap analysis when creating a title. The suggestions from a generative AI tool can help you explore other directions you might want to go with your title tag.

Figure 4-6 shows the results from Microsoft Copilot when asked to suggest alternative title tags for an existing page.

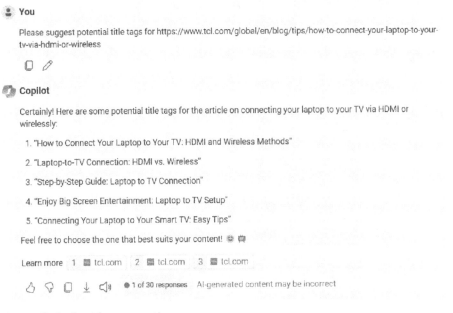

**You**

Please suggest potential title tags for https://www.tcl.com/global/en/blog/tips/how-to-connect-your-laptop-to-your-tv-via-hdmi-or-wireless

**Copilot**

Certainly! Here are some potential title tags for the article on connecting your laptop to your TV via HDMI or wirelessly:

1. "How to Connect Your Laptop to Your TV: HDMI and Wireless Methods"

2. "Laptop-to-TV Connection: HDMI vs. Wireless"

3. "Step-by-Step Guide: Laptop to TV Connection"

4. "Enjoy Big Screen Entertainment: Laptop to TV Setup"

5. "Connecting Your Laptop to Your Smart TV: Easy Tips"

Feel free to choose the one that best suits your content! 😊 📺

Learn more  1  📖 tcl.com   2  📖 tcl.com   3  📖 tcl.com

● 1 of 30 responses   AI-generated content may be incorrect

*Figure 4-6. Copilot title tag suggestions*

The response provides five different options for consideration. While these title tags don't account for search volume, Copilot shows what it thinks the page is about.

## DRAFTING META DESCRIPTIONS

The SEO community has long believed that *meta descriptions*—a brief paragraph in the head section of your website that describes a page's content, which Google sometimes uses as the description for your pages' listings in the SERPs—are not a direct input to search ranking algorithms (meaning that keyword usage in the meta description doesn't affect rankings). That said, we've always suspected that CTRs of results are a factor, and the Google leak confirms that Google does closely track users' click behavior within search results.

We should also treat meta descriptions as a ranking factor because they are often used by Google as the description of your listing in the search results. If you write a compelling meta description that stands out from the descriptions of other search listings, you can increase your CTR.

### Note

Google sometimes chooses to display your meta descriptions, and other times it extracts descriptive text from the document, based on what Google believes creates a stronger match between the user query and the document content.

In Figure 4-7, you can see how attracting more clicks from the search results can potentially influence rankings. For example, your page is ranked number three in a search result, and the expected CTR for position three is 4.5%. If your page is clicked on only 3.6% of the time, chances are high that its ranking will be demoted. Similarly, if that same page is clicked on 6.1% of the time, your page may be moved up in the search results.

| Position | Expected CTR |
|----------|--------------|
| 1 | 9.5% |
| 2 | 3.4% |
| 3 | 2.3% |
| 4 | 1.6% |
| 5 | 0.9% |
| 6 | 0.7% |
| 7 | 0.5% |
| 8 | 0.5% |
| 9 | 0.3% |
| 10 | 0.2% |

← *If you rank in position 3 and your click-through rate (CTR) is 1.8%, your ranking position may be lowered*

*Figure 4-7. Search position versus CTR*

Note that the expected CTR shown in Figure 4-7 is just sample data, and the expected CTR performance likely varies significantly based on the user query. With changes in the market due to the advent of generative AI tools like ChatGPT, Gemini, Copilot, Claude, and Google's integration of AIOs into the search results, your CTR will likely be significantly lower. Once Google integrates AI Mode in its search results, these clickthrough rates may decline even further.

Generating titles that attract user clicks is one of the more intriguing ways that generative AI can help SEO practitioners. The key is to ask the tool to write a meta description that users will find compelling. If you can do this well, it can lead to a higher CTR and even higher rankings.

As in all the exercises in this chapter, how you craft your prompt is a key component of success. Here is a suggestion for how you might initially structure a prompt to request a meta description:

> Write five new meta descriptions for https://www.meetboston.com/events/festivals-and-annual-events/boston-marathon/history/. The meta description should provide users with a compelling reason to click on the search listing in Google for the search query "history of the Boston Marathon." The target audience is people potentially interested in traveling to Boston as tourists.

Figure 4-8 shows what happens when you enter that query into Gemini.

Sure, here are five new meta descriptions for https://www.meetboston.com/events/festivals-and-annual-events/boston-marathon/history/ for the search query "history of the Boston Marathon":

1. Run through history at the Boston Marathon, the world's oldest annual marathon.

2. Discover the inspiring journey of the Boston Marathon, from its humble beginnings to its global acclaim.

3. Immerse yourself in the rich tradition of the Boston Marathon, a Boston must-see for any tourist.

4. Feel the excitement of the Boston Marathon, a race that celebrates athleticism, inclusivity, and community.

5. Unleash your inner runner and learn about the Boston Marathon, a race that will leave you breathless.

*Figure 4-8. Sample meta descriptions from Gemini*

These suggestions provide a range of things to consider in optimizing a meta description. When updating the meta descriptions for your website, you may want to do your critical pages one at a time, with unique descriptions. Then for larger-scale projects (for example, if you have one thousand pages you want to update), you may want to generate only one meta description per page. Then perform a human review of them all in bulk before publishing.

---

### Case Study: Updating Titles and Meta Descriptions in Bulk

Dallas-based digital marketing agency RankHammer provided us with a case study using ChatGPT-4 to edit the titles and meta descriptions for more than 1,500 pages of a lead-generation site. RankHammer set up a process to get ChatGPT-4 to make suggested recommendations in blocks of 10 pages at a time. After the pages were pushed live, RankHammer tracked the CTR from the SERPs to those pages. As you can see in Figure 4-9, there was a 12% increase in CTR. The changes made to the title tags and meta descriptions by ChatGPT-4 made a significant difference in the CTR.

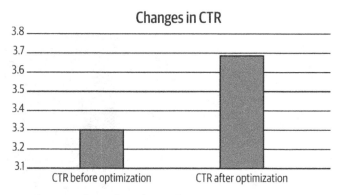

*Figure 4-9. CTR gains from title and meta description optimizations*

---

### IDENTIFYING CONTENT GAPS

Using generative AI to help identify content gaps in your existing pages is potentially a very high ROI activity. ChatGPT-4o, Gemini, and Copilot are all excellent tools for this application. They can rapidly identify areas that are missing or that can use deeper coverage than you currently have.

An example prompt might be:

*Provide a content gap analysis of: https://www.britannica.com/topic/European-Union. Key areas of focus should be: (1) the legal system and its significance; (2) the European economic community. Suggest how the content can be improved in those areas and provide links to related resources.*

Figure 4-10 shows a portion of the response from Gemini to this prompt.

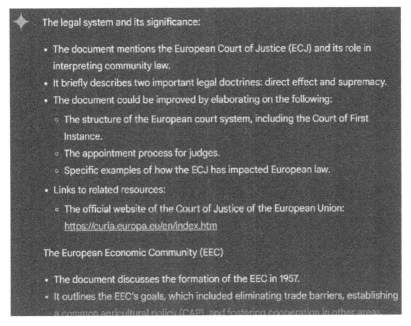

The legal system and its significance:

- The document mentions the European Court of Justice (ECJ) and its role in interpreting community law.
- It briefly describes two important legal doctrines: direct effect and supremacy.
- The document could be improved by elaborating on the following:
  - The structure of the European court system, including the Court of First Instance.
  - The appointment process for judges.
  - Specific examples of how the ECJ has impacted European law.
- Links to related resources:
  - The official website of the Court of Justice of the European Union: https://curia.europa.eu/en/index.htm

The European Economic Community (EEC)

- The document discusses the formation of the EEC in 1957.
- It outlines the EEC's goals, which included eliminating trade barriers, establishing a common agricultural policy (CAP) and fostering cooperation in other areas.

*Figure 4-10. Gemini output for content gap analysis prompt*

You can see the references to the current document and its content, followed by suggestions for content that could be added. You can also see links to references that can be used for more research. One way you might want to tweak the sample prompt is to ask for multiple references for each topic area. This will help you deepen your knowledge before writing anything to fill the suggested gaps.

## GENERATING DATABASE-DRIVEN CONTENT

Using facts and figures you pull from a database, you can reduce the chance of AI-generated errors. This is especially more effective if you provide generative AI with information that you've curated and fact-checked yourself. As discussed in Chapter 3, letting generative AI create content for you without human review is ill-advised. Expert human review should always be included. However, the more constrained the generative AI tool is, the less likely it is to make errors.

One example would be if you have a retail chain with one hundred locations and want some simple text at the top of every location's page. Let's work on three locations at a time to keep things simple. Bear in mind that your generative AI tool can't access your database directly, so you'll need to do that programmatically. In our fictitious example, we'll extract data for three locations and incorporate that data into our sample prompt shown here:

> *Rephrase the following paragraph for three different locations of Powerful Pizza but avoid repetition while keeping its meaning. Use the following information for each location:*
>
> > *Location 1:*
> >
> > > *Address: 21 Pizza Place, Austin Texas.*
> > >
> > > *Hours: M-F 11:00 AM to 10:00 PM. Sat/Sun: 11:00 AM to 9:00 PM.*
> > >
> > > *Proprietor: Lisa James*
> > >
> > > *Specialties: Pepperoni, Meat Lovers*
> >
> > *Location 2:*
> >
> > > *Address: 2134 Roundabout Way, San Jose California.*
> > >
> > > *Hours: Mon-Sat 10:00 AM to 11:00 PM, Sun 11:00 AM to 10:00 PM*
> > >
> > > *Proprietor: Donald Thompson*
> > >
> > > *Specialties: Double Cheese, California-Style Pizza*
> >
> > *Location 3:*
> >
> > > *Address: 21 Prometheus Promenade, Minneapolis Minnesota.*
> > >
> > > *Hours: M-S 11:00 AM to 10:00 PM, Sun 11:30 AM to 10:00 PM*
> > >
> > > *Proprietor: Susan Belinsky*
> > >
> > > *Specialties: Mushroom and Onion, Pineapple*
>
> *Also use the following template as an example of what we're looking for. Vary the text from location to location but use the template as an example of the desired length and tone:*
>
> > *Powerful Pizza offers some of the finest pizzas available anywhere in the United States. We use only natural ingredients from local farms in all of our pies. Popular pizzas in our stores include cheese, pepperoni, pineapple, and meat lovers.*

*We always strive to be price competitive, but the quality of our pizzas and service matters most to our customers. We'll treat you like a long-lost friend when you come to visit us. We look forward to seeing you soon!*

Figure 4-11 shows the content created for the first two locations using this prompt.

Location 1: Austin, Texas

Powerful Pizza at 21 Pizza Place in Austin, Texas, managed by Lisa James, serves some of the best pizzas you'll find anywhere. Open Monday to Friday from 11:00 AM to 10:00 PM and weekends from 11:00 AM to 9:00 PM, we use only natural ingredients sourced from local farms. Our specialty pizzas include the popular Pepperoni and Meat Lovers. We focus on providing exceptional quality and service, all at competitive prices. When you visit us, you'll be treated like family. We can't wait to welcome you soon!

Location 2: San Jose, California

At Powerful Pizza, located at 2134 Roundabout Way in San Jose, California, proprietor Donald Thompson brings you a delightful pizza experience. We're open from 10:00 AM to 11:00 PM Monday through Saturday and 11:00 AM to 10:00 PM on Sundays. Our pizzas are made with natural, locally sourced ingredients, and our specialties include Double Cheese and California-Style Pizza. We are committed to offering great value without compromising on quality and service. Visit us, and we'll make sure you feel right at home. See you soon!

*Figure 4-11. Initial example of database-driven content generation*

As you can see, the sample responses are pretty good, but there's room for improvement. There are many other things that you could do to enhance this process, such as:

- Provide more than one sample description template to broaden the range of approaches for the generative AI tool.
- Include other information related to the stores, such as parking, in the database and in your template(s).
- Provide follow-on prompts to tweak the tone and structure of the output to better fit what you're looking for.

Because we constrained the information used by the generative AI tool, it has a much smaller chance of making mistakes or using unusual word choices. That makes for a great start. Nonetheless, we still suggest that you give any database-driven content you create using generative AI a review before publishing it.

## GENERATING FAQS

You can use generative AI to create lists of frequently asked questions (FAQs) for your site. There are multiple ways that you can use these lists of FAQs, including:

- Publishing them as FAQs on your web pages
- Treating them as suggestions for additional content in your existing articles
- Using them as potential new article topics

An example prompt to start with might be "Please provide FAQs for best places to see in Boston." Figure 4-12 shows how Claude responded to the prompt.

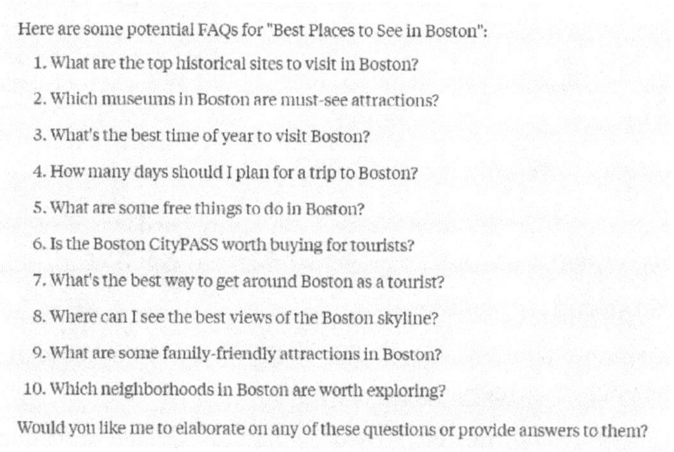

Here are some potential FAQs for "Best Places to See in Boston":

1. What are the top historical sites to visit in Boston?

2. Which museums in Boston are must-see attractions?

3. What's the best time of year to visit Boston?

4. How many days should I plan for a trip to Boston?

5. What are some free things to do in Boston?

6. Is the Boston CityPASS worth buying for tourists?

7. What's the best way to get around Boston as a tourist?

8. Where can I see the best views of the Boston skyline?

9. What are some family-friendly attractions in Boston?

10. Which neighborhoods in Boston are worth exploring?

Would you like me to elaborate on any of these questions or provide answers to them?

*Figure 4-12. Initial FAQs for best places to see in Boston from Claude*

These are pretty good, but perhaps you decided that you wanted 20 FAQs. Ask your generative AI tool to "provide 10 more FAQs." Figure 4-13 shows how Claude responded to that query.

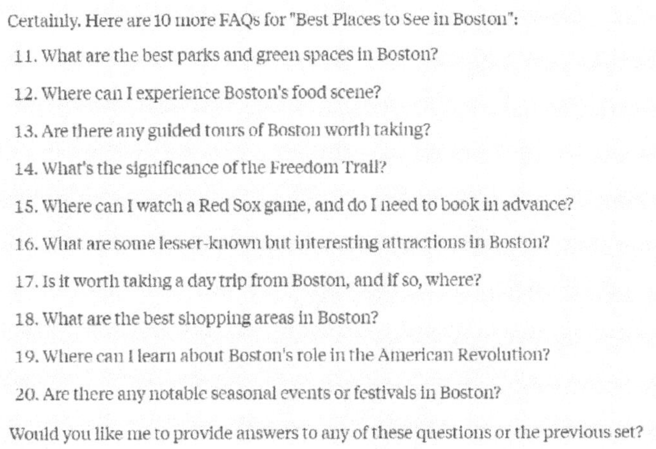

Certainly. Here are 10 more FAQs for "Best Places to See in Boston":

11. What are the best parks and green spaces in Boston?

12. Where can I experience Boston's food scene?

13. Are there any guided tours of Boston worth taking?

14. What's the significance of the Freedom Trail?

15. Where can I watch a Red Sox game, and do I need to book in advance?

16. What are some lesser-known but interesting attractions in Boston?

17. Is it worth taking a day trip from Boston, and if so, where?

18. What are the best shopping areas in Boston?

19. Where can I learn about Boston's role in the American Revolution?

20. Are there any notable seasonal events or festivals in Boston?

Would you like me to provide answers to any of these questions or the previous set?

*Figure 4-13. Additional FAQs for best places to see in Boston from Claude*

This is a simple but excellent use of generative AI. You can use these FAQs to provide supplemental content on an existing page, to create new pages for each FAQ, or a mix of both.

**Tip**

We'll discuss how to use generative AI to create FAQ schema code for an existing set of FAQs in Chapter 5.

## SOURCING DATA AND STATISTICS

Generative AI also has strong capabilities for sourcing data and statistics. This is an approach that can be used to improve the quality of content on your site, either by integrating it into content you're writing from scratch or to bolster content you've already published.

Here is an example of a sample prompt:

*Provide data and statistics for an article on the battle of Stiklestad. Provide URLs for sources for each statistic provided.*

Figure 4-14 shows Copilot's response to this query.

Certainly! The **Battle of Stiklestad** took place in 1030 and is one of Norway's most famous battles. Here are the key statistics:

1. **Strength:**

   ○ King Olaf II's forces: Approximately **6,600** soldiers [1].

   ○ "Farmer Army" (opposing force): Comprised mainly of peasants, with over **14,000** fighters [1].

2. **Casualties and Losses:**

   ○ Olaf II's forces: Around **4,200** casualties.

   ○ "Farmer Army": Suffered approximately **4,600** losses [1].

The authenticity of the battle remains debated, but contemporary sources suggest that Olaf II was either murdered by his own people or ambushed [1][2][3]. For more details, you can explore the following sources:

- Wikipedia
- Life in Norway
- The Viking Herald [2][4][5]. Let me know if you need further information! 😊

*Figure 4-14. Copilot response on statistics on the battle of Stiklestad*

These results already provide some great information, but you can further enhance them by asking additional prompts requesting more stats.

## Warning

Always double-check data sources and make sure the numbers and statistics are indeed correct before final publishing. Sometimes, generative AI makes up content (including stats) to cover a gap in its training data. One way to fact-check AI-generated content is to instruct the AI to include references in its output. A human reviewer can then check the source to validate information.

## CREATING A LIST OF RELEVANT QUESTIONS

There are many ways you can use AI to help you create new content or enhance existing content. One way to do this is to use AI to make a list of relevant questions on your topic. For example, you might try a prompt like "Create a list of questions related to states' rights in the United States." Figure 4-15 shows 14 of the 20 questions that ChatGPT-4o provided in response to this prompt.

Certainly! Here is a list of questions related to states' rights in the United States:

1. What are states' rights and how are they defined in the U.S. Constitution?
2. How does the Tenth Amendment of the U.S. Constitution relate to states' rights?
3. What historical events have significantly impacted the concept of states' rights in the U.S.?
4. How did the Civil War and Reconstruction era influence states' rights?
5. What is the significance of the Supremacy Clause in the context of states' rights?
6. How have Supreme Court decisions shaped the balance between state and federal powers?
7. What role did states' rights play in the Civil Rights Movement?
8. How do states' rights affect modern debates on issues like healthcare, education, and environmental regulation?
9. What are some examples of conflicts between state laws and federal laws?
10. How do states' rights impact the implementation of federal policies at the state level?
11. What are the arguments for and against states having more autonomy from the federal government?
12. How do states' rights influence the distribution of power in the federal system of government?
13. What are some key legislative acts that have expanded or restricted states' rights?
14. How do states' rights impact the administration of elections in the United States?

*Figure 4-15. Relevant questions generated by ChatGPT-4o*

This type of list can be used in several different ways:

- As a potential list of topic ideas for new pages to be created
- As input to topics that should be covered in a piece of content
- As ideas for FAQs to be added to one or more pages

## SUMMARIZING CONTENT

Creating or updating content often requires reading through many other sources of information on the topic. This can be a tedious task and is another area where generative AI can help. For example, instead of reading a one-hundred-page whitepaper to find out if it has the information you need, you can have AI summarize it for you and even tell you where to find specific information. To demonstrate this, we'll use Claude to summarize a whitepaper. Claude can't read live web pages, but it can accept attachments such as PDFs.

Figure 4-16 shows a Claude screen that has the option to add content. Click on that link and then attach the content you want Claude to read. Then make the following prompt: "Summarize the contents of the attached document." For this exercise, we attached a PDF of Google's "Decoding Decisions: Making Sense of the Messy Middle" whitepaper (*https://oreil.ly/BTW3L*).

*Figure 4-16. Adding an attachment to Claude*

Once you do this, Claude will provide a summary of the content. You can see example output for a summary of the whitepaper in Figure 4-17.

This document appears to be a comprehensive report titled "Decoding Decisions: Making sense of the messy middle" produced by Google in collaboration with The Behavioural Architects. The report explores how consumers make purchasing decisions in the digital age, focusing on what the authors call the "messy middle" - the complex space of abundant information and choice that shoppers navigate between trigger and purchase.

Key points from the report include:

1. A new model of consumer decision-making is proposed, featuring exploration and evaluation loops that consumers cycle through before making a purchase.

2. The report identifies six key cognitive biases that influence decision-making: category heuristics, authority bias, social proof, power of now, scarcity bias, and power of free.

3. Extensive research was conducted, including literature reviews, analysis of Google Trends data, and large-scale simulated shopping experiments across 31 product categories.

4. The experiments revealed that even strong brand preferences can be disrupted by effectively leveraging behavioral science principles.

5. The report offers implications and recommendations for both established and challenger brands, emphasizing the importance of brand presence, intelligent use of behavioral science, and optimizing the path to purchase.

*Figure 4-17. Claude output for content summarization*

As you can see, using generative AI to summarize content can help streamline your content research and generation process.

## CREATING A LIST OF TRENDS

Another interesting area where generative AI can help with content development is in identifying current trends for a market. This can be of great value to your writer in coming up with ideas for new articles or for how to enhance existing articles on your site. When generating a list of trends, it's a good idea to prompt different tools to give you a more comprehensive view. Each tool may cite different trends, so combining the output from multiple tools will provide you with a more inclusive list.

Figure 4-18 shows an example of the Gemini response to the prompt "Generate a simple list of blockchain technology trends."

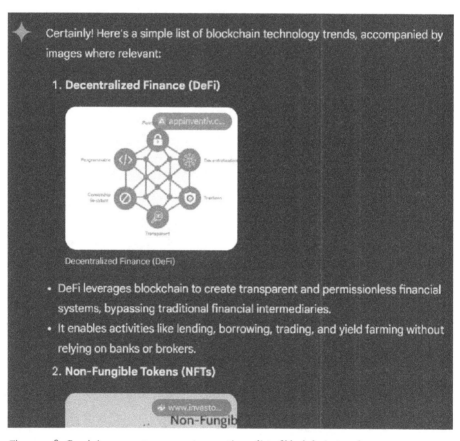

*Figure 4-18. Gemini response to a prompt requesting a list of blockchain trends*

You'll see that the response includes a fair amount of detail. In total, Gemini provided seven trends, all of which included images and descriptions. In contrast, the response from ChatGPT-4o is shown in Figure 4-19.

 Here's a simple list of current trends in blockchain technology:

1. Decentralized Finance (DeFi) Growth

2. Central Bank Digital Currencies (CBDCs)

3. Non-Fungible Tokens (NFTs)

4. Blockchain Interoperability

5. Green Blockchain Initiatives (Energy Efficiency)

6. Decentralized Autonomous Organizations (DAOs)

7. Layer 2 Scaling Solutions (e.g., Rollups)

8. Blockchain in Supply Chain Management

9. Regulatory Frameworks for Cryptocurrencies

10. Blockchain Integration with IoT (Internet of Things)

These trends reflect the expanding use cases and innovations within the blockchain space.

*Figure 4-19. ChatGPT output for trends in blockchain technology*

You'll notice that the response to the prompt is much simpler than Gemini's response. You can try to get ChatGPT-4o to produce a similar level of detail as Gemini with a revised prompt such as:

*Provide a simple list of trends for blockchain technology. Include short descriptions and images for each trend.*

This produced short descriptions for each trend but only one summary image for the overall response. If you want one image per trend, you should further modify your prompt to ChatGPT-4o to request that.

As always, increasing your chances of getting the results you want requires tuning your prompts and trying different platforms. If one platform is not giving you the response you're looking for, you can try other platforms to see if they provide better results. When creating a list of trends, make sure you're using a generative AI tool that has web-browsing capability to ensure that you capture the latest trends. We will discuss advanced use cases, including using AI agents to perform trend analysis, in Chapter 6.

## Using AI Throughout Content Development

So far in this chapter, we've discussed many ways that generative AI can assist in the process of creating high-quality content. Now it's time to bring it all together.

Let's consider what an AI-supported process might look like if the task at hand is creating a new piece of content. We'll start with the steps you might take to decide on an article topic and then conduct research to inform the contents of an article:

*Generate topic ideas and suggested titles*
This provides your SME a great start in the process of developing new content. If you've already published many related articles on a topic, include a list of the existing article titles as part of the prompt and clarify that you're looking for new subjects. This can help steer your generative AI tool away from suggesting topics that you've already covered. Let's assume after this step that you decide on a new article topic you want to cover.

*List relevant questions for your selected topic*
This is another prompt that helps you understand what questions users have. It can inform key subtopics that you want to cover in your article.

*Draft outlines for your selected topic*
When you create new content, your first step is probably to draft an outline of what you want to include in your page. Better still, use generative AI to create three outlines, and your SME can take the best from each of them and merge them into one.

*Summarize competitive content for your selected topic*
Ask generative AI to summarize the content of competing articles on your selected topic. This is a great way to gather more information for a high-quality outline for your content.

*Summarize topical content for your selected topic*
This is the same concept as competitive content summarization but for pages that compete in the SERPs, which aren't direct competitors.

*Identify key trends*

Building out lists of key trends related to your space can provide more valuable ideas for new content or enhancements to existing content.

*Find facts and statistics related to your selected topic*

This is a very effective way to add valuable data to your content. Take some of the most important content on your site and then pull related facts and stats to make it even better.

*Generate FAQs for your selected topic*

Having a list of frequently asked questions and their answers on your key pages is a great way to add value to your content. This is one way to address many of the long-tail questions people have.

Once you've completed all these steps, your writer will have a rich array of information to consider and leverage when creating the content. You may only want to go through these steps for your most important pages, but for those pages you will:

- Speed up the process of creating content

- Reduce the overall cost of creating the content by fully enabling your writer up front

- Improve the quality of the resulting content

For less important pieces of content, you may choose to implement a subset of the steps. For example, perhaps you get generative AI to assist with providing topic ideas, relevant user questions, draft outlines, and FAQs. This is already a lot of information to equip your writer with input for creating a new piece of content.

After the piece has been written, you can use generative AI to perform further tasks, such as writing draft meta descriptions and title tags.

For existing content that you want to update, there are also numerous steps you can take. These include some of the steps from the preceding list: generating a list of relevant questions, identifying trends, and researching interesting facts and statistics. You can also add these two steps:

*Competitive gap analysis*

    For existing content, ask generative AI to summarize the topics covered by competing pages but not by your page. This should provide numerous ideas for how to enhance your existing content.

*Topical gap analysis*

    This is the same concept as the competitive gap analysis but for pages that compete in the SERPs but aren't direct competitors.

For many of these use cases, consider having the model you're using provide multiple versions of its work, review them, and give you a final recommendation. You may also want to try to mix and match the different models; for example, have ChatGPT-4o generate two versions, optimize its own output, and make recommendations, and then have Claude or Gemini take that as input and optimize it further. In addition to catching more errors, this advanced technique can be especially helpful for things that the models approach differently. For example, ChatGPT is known for being more verbose and lacking tone, unlike Claude, which can be more succinct and sound more human.

You don't necessarily need to pursue all the ideas that we discussed in this chapter, but putting many of them into place will help you improve your content quality, reduce costs, and increase throughput. It may take some time for your writers and SMEs to get used to a modified process and to maximize the benefits of incorporating some of these steps into the process. If people are resistant to changing an established process, inform them how the modifications will make their lives easier.

## Conclusion

Throughout the chapter, we've provided numerous examples of ways you can use generative AI to improve your content development process. These methods offer great potential to save costs, increase throughput, and improve quality all at the same time. The approaches suggested in this chapter are also designed to leverage the strengths of generative AI tools while minimizing the risks associated with asking them to do more than they're capable of doing. This is why we consistently stress the importance of human review of AI outputs before deploying those outputs.

In Chapter 5, we'll discuss the ways that you can use generative AI to help with a variety of SEO tasks. In the same way as we did in this chapter, we'll provide approaches that minimize risks and maximize benefits.

# 5

# Using AI to Assist with Technical SEO

In Chapter 4, we discussed many ways that generative AI can help you create new content. We also talked about how you can use generative AI as a brainstorming partner for your writers and SMEs, which can help them work more effectively.

In this chapter, we'll follow a similar theme. Your SEO team has a lot on their plate, and technical SEO tasks can be time-consuming. You can use generative AI to make their job easier and improve the quality of their work. As with creating content, you will need to check the output of your generative AI tools. For example, you might have a developer review code written by your tool or have an experienced SEO practitioner review keywords that your tool has recommended.

Throughout this chapter, we'll show you many ways that you can improve the productivity of technical SEO work and empower your staff to be more efficient. The benefits of using generative AI to do this work include increasing the throughput of completing the work, reducing costs, and potentially even decreasing errors. This idea of reducing errors with AI may seem counterintuitive, given the need for a thorough review of generative AI outputs, but your SEO team and developers can make errors, too. Employing both generative AI and humans increases the potential of reducing the total number of errors in these tasks.

## Keyword Research

Keyword research is a common technical SEO task that involves researching what people are searching for. This can help you decide what new content you need to create or come up with enhancements to existing content. You can use tools such as Semrush, Ahrefs, seoClarity, BrightEdge, Conductor, and others to get data on potential keywords for your site.

## SUGGESTING KEYWORDS

Keyword research tools typically require you to provide an initial seed keyword as input and then give you a list of closely related keywords and their estimated search volume. However, these tools tend to be narrowly focused in how they make suggestions, and they don't always provide a view of concepts that are closely related to your seed keyword. For example, Figure 5-1 shows the output from Semrush's Keyword Magic Tool after giving it the seed keyword "ultrasound technician."

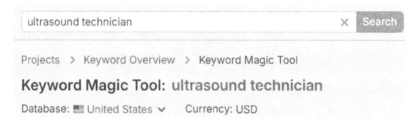

*Figure 5-1. Example seed keyword input into Semrush's Keyword Magic Tool*

The example output is shown in Figure 5-2. Note how all the results include the seed keyword—for example, you don't see any keywords based on variants of *sonography*, which is a synonym of *ultrasound*. Seeing such variants might prompt your content team to consider other topics that are of great interest to your site visitors. Generative AI can make discovering these variants a lot easier.

Imagine you are working for a company that provides training courses for medical personnel. You want to create content to increase the visibility of your company in searches for training providers. Using a tool like the Keyword Magic Tool from Semrush is a great place to start. But let's consider what happens when you decide to create some content to help you promote your training materials for becoming an ultrasound technician. Refer to Figure 5-1 for entering the seed keyword in Semrush's Keyword Magic Tool and Figure 5-2 for the output provided by the tool.

All keywords: **7.6K**   Total volume: **227,000**   Average KD: **31%**                     + Add to list   C   ⚙   ⊥

| | Keyword | Intent | Volume ⇌ | KD % | CPC (USD) | SF | Updated |
|---|---|---|---|---|---|---|---|
| ⊕ | ultrasound technician salary ⊟ | I | 22.2K | 40 ◉ | 3.72 🔍 | 3 | 2 weeks C |
| ⊕ | ultrasound technician school ⊟ | C | 14.8K | 40 ◉ | 2.84 🔍 | 4 | 2 weeks C |
| ⊕ | ultrasound technician ⊟ | I | 12.1K | 51 ● | 3.05 🔍 | 4 | 2 weeks C |
| ⊕ | how to become an ultrasound technician ⊟ | I | 9.9K | 51 ● | 2.83 🔍 | 3 | 2 weeks C |
| ⊕ | ultrasound technician programs ⊟ | C | 6.6K | 47 ◉ | 2.61 🔍 | 5 | 2 weeks C |
| ⊕ | ultrasound technician programs near me ⊟ | T | 5.4K | 48 ◉ | 2.88 🔍 | 5 | 2 weeks C |
| ⊕ | ultrasound technician schools near me ⊟ | T | 4.4K | 46 ◉ | 2.88 🔍 | 3 | 2 weeks C |
| ⊕ | how much do an ultrasound technician make ⊟ | I | 2.4K | 40 ◉ | 0.00 🔍 | 3 | 2 weeks C |
| ⊕ | how to become a ultrasound technician ⊟ | I | 2.4K | 47 ◉ | 3.26 🔍 | 3 | 2 weeks C |
| ⊕ | how to become ultrasound technician ⊟ | I | 1.9K | 50 ● | 3.26 🔍 | 3 | 2 weeks C |
| ⊕ | ultrasound technician | I  C | 1.9K | 30 ◉ | 3.42 🔍 | 2 | 2 weeks C |

*Figure 5-2. Example output from Semrush's Keyword Magic Tool*

The list in Figure 5-2 includes many keywords that are simple derivatives of the original seed keyword. This is highly valuable data but may not cover the full scope of the related topics. Semrush has a feature that enables you to see related keywords that broaden this scope, which is also valuable to use. In addition to this list, you may want to obtain more data to widen the list of keywords more. This is where generative AI tools can help, and we'll illustrate how to use them next.

Let's use a simple example prompt: "Suggest important keywords related to becoming an ultrasound technician." Figure 5-3 shows a portion of what ChatGPT-4o provided in response to this prompt.

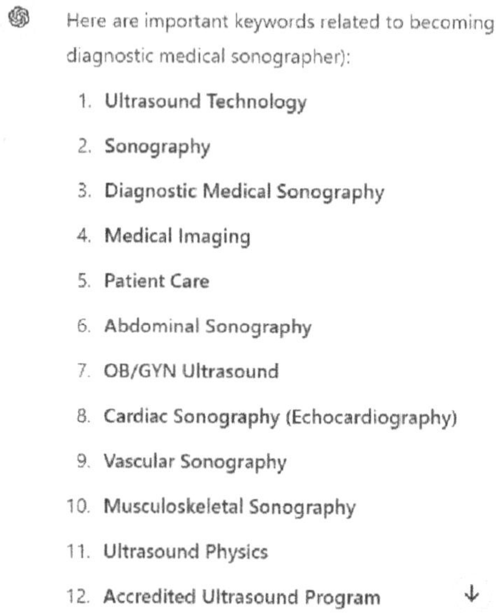

Here are important keywords related to becoming an ultrasound technician (also known as a diagnostic medical sonographer):

1. Ultrasound Technology

2. Sonography

3. Diagnostic Medical Sonography

4. Medical Imaging

5. Patient Care

6. Abdominal Sonography

7. OB/GYN Ultrasound

8. Cardiac Sonography (Echocardiography)

9. Vascular Sonography

10. Musculoskeletal Sonography

11. Ultrasound Physics

12. Accredited Ultrasound Program

*Figure 5-3. ChatGPT output snippet*

The full response in Figure 5-3 contained 30 keyword suggestions. You'll notice a wide range of related keywords, a broader list than what the Keyword Magic Tool provided. The Keyword Magic Tool is very beneficial to SEO practitioners, and you should obtain this data from the SEO tool of your choice, but generative AI supplements this research with a wider range of suggestions.

## Note

Keyword research is less helpful for ranking in generative AI tools, but it is still helpful in the traditional SEO search results.

## GROUPING KEYWORDS BY SEARCH INTENT

Once you have a list of keywords for your page, you can take your research further by classifying the keywords by their search intent. Knowing the user's intent can help you determine what kind of page you should create to fulfill their need and draw them to your page.

For example, keywords with commercial search intent, such as "Boston Celtics gear," indicate that a user might want a page that helps them browse and purchase Boston Celtics merchandise. Keywords with transactional intent, such as "Boston Celtics tickets," indicate that the user wants to go directly into the process of purchasing something. Keywords with informational search intent, such as "Boston Celtics draft picks," indicate that the user would like to see an article about the team's most recent picks.

Here's where generative AI can help. You can prompt a generative AI tool to take an existing keyword list and group the terms by search intent. Figure 5-4 shows an example prompt asking a generative AI tool to group keywords by search intent.

**Classify the following keyword list in groups based on their search intent, whether commercial, transactional, or informational:**

| | |
|---|---|
| Boston Celtics history | Boston Celtics parking |
| Boston Celtics NBA championships | Boston Celtics trade rumors |
| Boston Celtics website | Boston Celtics draft picks |
| Boston Celtics schedule 2023 | Boston Celtics highlights |
| Boston Celtics players | Boston Celtics game results |
| Boston Celtics coach | Boston Celtics playoffs |
| Boston Celtics gear | Boston Celtics standings |
| Boston Celtics tickets | Boston Celtics scores |
| Buy Boston Celtics tickets | Boston Celtics tickets |
| Boston Celtics stats | Boston Celtics merchandise |

*Figure 5-4. Prompting generative AI to group keywords by intent*

We tested this prompt in Microsoft Copilot, and Figure 5-5 shows the results.

*Figure 5-5. Copilot output grouping keywords by intent*

The results are mostly accurate, though there are some items we might question. For example, "Boston Celtics Website" probably doesn't belong in the transactional category. We've seen similar errors with the other major generative AI tools. This mistake reaffirms the importance of human review of generative AI output, but reviewing it is quick and easy in this example.

### GROUPING KEYWORDS BY SEMANTIC RELEVANCE

Another task you can use generative AI tools to help you with is categorizing keywords into logical groupings. This can be useful after you've put together a long list of keywords and you want to sort them by category before turning them over to a content team to create new or enhance existing content. Grouping the keyword set by semantic relevance can make it easier to assign the keywords to the right staff and for the staff to more easily see related keywords together. Imagine, for example, that you're doing this exercise with a thousand keywords! Using generative AI, this can be set up as an automated process to pull in keyword data and classify it.

Figure 5-6 shows an example prompt asking a generative AI tool to group keywords by relevance.

## Cluster the following keywords into groups based on their semantic relevance:

| | |
|---|---|
| Bookshelves | Pine |
| Chop saw | Plywood |
| Coffee table | Poplar |
| Desk | Redwood |
| Dining room table | Router |
| End table | Sanding block |
| Mahogany | Sandpaper |
| Maple | Table saw |
| Miter saw | |

*Figure 5-6. Prompting generative AI to group keywords by relevance*

We tested this prompt with Claude AI, and Figure 5-7 shows the results.

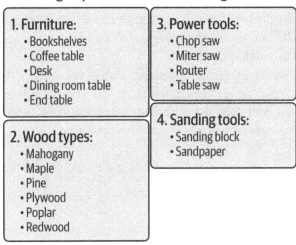

*Figure 5-7. Claude output grouping keywords by relevance*

Once the task is complete, you can perform a quick human review and then pass the classified keywords over to your SEO or content team for further analysis. You can also ask the generative AI tool to explain the reasoning for its categorizations. When asked, Claude explained its categorizations as follows:

*This clustering groups the keywords based on their relationships:*

*Furniture items that could be built*

*Types of wood that could be used in woodworking*

*Power tools commonly used in woodworking*

*Tools specifically used for sanding and finishing*

Overall, it did an excellent job with this task. Generative AI tools are less likely to make errors when performing classification tasks like these, but you should still review the output.

## Schema Markup

Writing schema markup code is another common technical SEO task. If you're not familiar with schema, what it does, and how it works, you can learn more about it from the Schema.org website (*https://schema.org*). Using different types of schema results in Google enhancing your SERP listings with special features, which can lead to a higher CTR.

Figure 5-8 shows an example of search results for a movie that have been enhanced by displaying detailed information on reviews (underlined in the image). Not only does this look nice, but it has also been shown to increase the CTR on the search listings that include this markup.

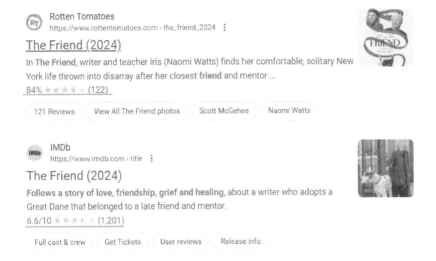

Figure 5-8. Example of how schema can improve SERP appearance

As we saw in Chapter 1, CTR in the SERPs can impact your rankings, so implementing Schema for content where Google uses it to enhance your search listings should be a high priority. You can learn more about the types of schema that affect Google's search listings in the Google Search documentation (*https:// oreil.ly/Z7pGe*).

## GENERATING AGGREGATERATING SCHEMA MARKUP

In Figure 5-8, you saw one example of a highly popular form of schema markup enhancing Google's SERP listings. This type of schema displays the aggregated review scores for all the reviews of a movie. The IMDb example shows an average score of 6.6 out of 10 for 1,201 reviews. Next, let's look at how to implement that. Figure 5-9 shows a sample prompt, including some review data to ask your generative AI tool of choice to implement the code that you would need to put in your web page to make this happen. Please note that in this example, we made an error in what we named the AggregateRating schema, but the AI understood the prompt anyway.

Please implement AggregateReview Schema code for the following data.

Type: Movie
Image: "https://www.example.com/movie-image.jpg"
Name: The Friend
Aggregate Rating: 4.5
Total Ratings: 336

*Figure 5-9. Prompt to request Aggregate Rating schema*

Figure 5-10 shows what happens when we feed that prompt into ChatGPT-4o.

Sure! Here's the **AggregateRating Schema** in JSON-LD format based on your data:

```json
<script type="application/ld+json">
{
  "@context": "https://schema.org",
  "@type": "Movie",
  "name": "The Friend",
  "image": "https://www.example.com/movie-image.jpg",
  "aggregateRating": {
    "@type": "AggregateRating",
    "ratingValue": "4.5",
    "reviewCount": "336"
  }
}
</script>
```

This will properly mark up the movie and its aggregate review data for search engines. Would you like to add other details, such as the director, genre, or a description?

*Figure 5-10. Example of JSON-LD schema code provided by ChatGPT-4o*

Once you have this code and a developer on your team has reviewed it, the next step is to post the code on the appropriate page of your website. Since this particular piece of code is in JSON-LD format, it should be placed in the head section of the page. Note that you can also provide the desired type of schema markup code you want in your prompt. Potential types of schema code include JSON-LD, microdata, and RDFa. Which type of schema code you use is a development decision, but generative AI tools can help you write the code in any of these formats.

### GENERATING FAQPAGE SCHEMA MARKUP FROM A Q&A

One popular form of content to have on your website is a FAQs section. Currently, FAQs are used by Google to show a rich listing only for a website that is either government or health focused. Even if you don't operate one of those types of websites, FAQPage schema can still help Google better understand your content.

Creating this code can be a bit tricky, but generative AI can help you by writing a draft of the code. One way to have a generative AI tool create FAQPage schema code for you is by feeding it FAQ questions and answers that you have already written. Figure 5-11 shows an example of a prompt to request the creation of FAQPage schema markup.

## Generate the FAQPage schema markup for the following question and answer:

Q: *What are the ingredients for Loc Lac?*

A: 2 pounds of bite size beef cubes
4 tablespoons of oyster sauce
2 tablespoons of sugar
2 tablespoons of fish sauce
4 tablespoons of minced garlic
2 tablespoons of thick soy sauce
1 teaspoon of black pepper

*Figure 5-11. Prompt requesting FAQPage schema markup for an existing FAQ*

We fed this prompt into ChatGPT-4o to get our code. Figure 5-12 shows the output we received.

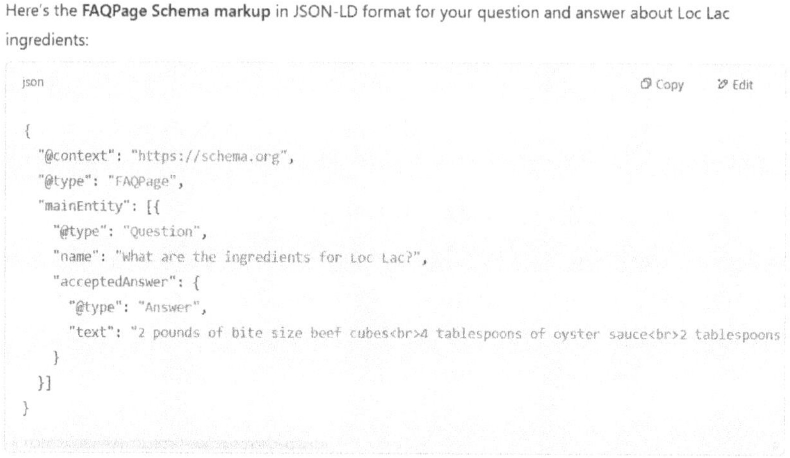

Here's the **FAQPage Schema markup** in JSON-LD format for your question and answer about Loc Lac ingredients:

```json
{
  "@context": "https://schema.org",
  "@type": "FAQPage",
  "mainEntity": [{
    "@type": "Question",
    "name": "What are the ingredients for Loc Lac?",
    "acceptedAnswer": {
      "@type": "Answer",
      "text": "2 pounds of bite size beef cubes<br>4 tablespoons of oyster sauce<br>2 tablespoons
    }
  }]
}
```

*Figure 5-12. FAQPage schema markup generated from an existing FAQ*

The code may look simple, but when you have a lot of these to do, starting with draft code can greatly streamline the work (as well as the tediousness of the task) for your developer. Of course, have your developer review the code for correctness before pushing it live.

## GENERATING FAQPAGE SCHEMA MARKUP FROM CONTENT

Now that you've seen how to generate FAQPage schema markup for an existing FAQ, let's take that one step further and have ChatGPT-4o generate FAQPage schema code from a block of content. Figure 5-13 shows what our prompt looks like.

### Generate the FAQPage schema for the following content:

*How many championships have the Boston Celtics won?*
The Celtics have won 17 NBA championships. They are tied with the Los Angeles Lakers, who have also won 17.

*Who is the greatest Boston Celtic player of all time?*
The greatest player in the history of the Celtics is Bill Russell. His Celtics teams won 11 NBA championships. An honorable mention goes to Larry Bird, who together with Magic Johnson helped transform the NBA.

*When was the last time the Celtics won the NBA championship?*
The Celtics won in 2008, beating the Lakers in 6 games, with a 131-92 series win. Paul Pierce was named the MVP of the finals.

*Which Boston Celtics coach had the most wins with the Celtics?*
The Boston Celtics coach with the most wins in franchise history is Red Auerbach, who coached the team for 16 seasons from 1950 to 1966. During his tenure as head coach, Auerbach led the Celtics to 938 regular-season wins and 99 playoff wins, including nine NBA championships.

*Figure 5-13. Prompt requesting FAQ and FAQPage schema markup from content*

Figure 5-14 shows us a portion of how ChatGPT4-o responds.

Below is an example of FAQPage Schema Markup in JSON-LD format for your provided content. You can include this script in the HTML of your page to help search engines understand and potentially display the FAQ in search results:

```html
<script type="application/ld+json">
{
  "@context": "https://schema.org",
  "@type": "FAQPage",
  "mainEntity": [
    {
      "@type": "Question",
      "name": "How many championships have the Boston Celtics won?",
      "acceptedAnswer": {
        "@type": "Answer",
        "text": "The Celtics have won 17 NBA championships. They are tied with the Los Ang
      }
    },
    {
      "@type": "Question",
      "name": "Who is the greatest Boston Celtic player of all time?",
      "acceptedAnswer": {
        "@type": "Answer",
```

*Figure 5-14. FAQ and FAQPage schema markup generated from content*

As with our previous FAQPage schema example, generative AI can take a task that might have taken your developer 30 minutes to an hour to complete and provide a draft as a starting place in just a few minutes. Then your developer can do a final review of the code, and once they've verified it, they can submit the code for publication on your site.

## HREFLANG

Many organizations create and publish web content that is meant to serve more than one language or country. For example, large brands may offer their products or services in a dozen or more countries. They can organize the various languages/countries on their website in many ways. Some examples of how they might organize this content include:

- On a separate website
- On a subdomain of their main domain
- In a subfolder of their main domain

It can be difficult for Google to parse all these variants, and there is the risk of Google treating them as duplicate content (meaning that Google wouldn't rank the pages it sees as duplicates). The purpose of hreflang tags is to help Google correctly parse all these pages and eliminate the chances of this happening.

However, hreflang tags can be tricky to implement. One important aspect of these tags is that you can have language tags alone or both language and country tags, but you aren't allowed to implement country-only tags. It's also important to use the correct standards for your language and country codes:

- Language codes: ISO 639-1
- Country codes: ISO 3166-1

Figure 5-15 shows how a proper hreflang implementation is supposed to work.

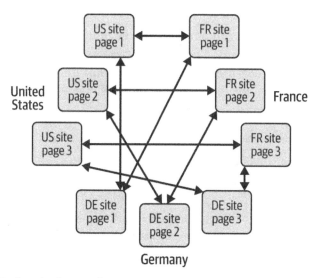

*Figure 5-15. Hreflang implementation*

As you can see, each country page needs to contain hreflag tags pointing to their sibling pages for all the alternative language (and country) versions of the same content. For example, if you have a sales product page in English, French, and German, you then need to create hreflang tags on each of these three pages that point to one another. This includes each page having a self-referential tag that points to itself.

This code can be tedious to write, and it's easy to make mistakes. However, you can use generative AI to write a draft of the code in one-quarter of the time it would take your developer, and then your developer can review the code and correct any issues they find. This may end up cutting your development time in half—that's a great savings!

For our example, we'll try the following prompt with Gemini:

*Generate the hreflang tags for the following pages:*

*Yourdomain.com, US, English*

*Yourdomain.com/uk/, UK, English*

*Yourdomain.com/ger/, Germany, German*

*Yourdomain.com, Switzerland, German*

*Yourdomain.com/che/, Switzerland, French*

*Yourdomain.com/che/, Switzerland, Italian*

*Yourdomain.com/che/, Switzerland, Romansh*

Figure 5-16 shows the reply from Gemini.

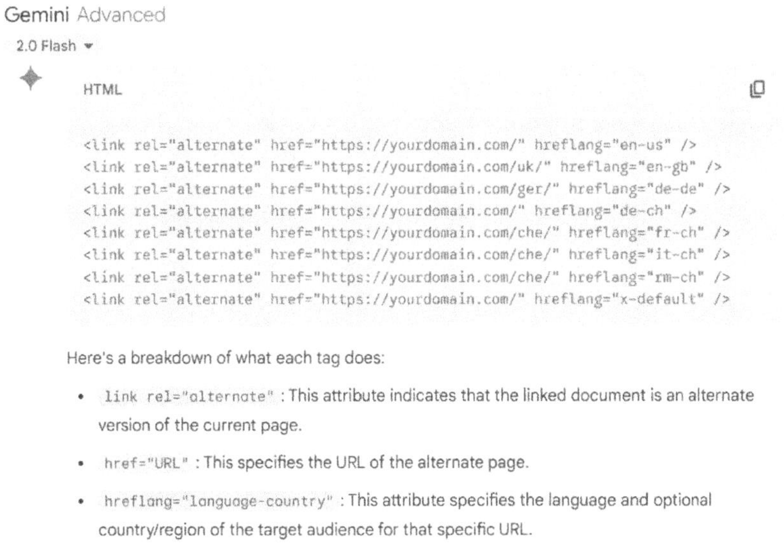

**Gemini** Advanced

2.0 Flash ▾

HTML

```html
<link rel="alternate" href="https://yourdomain.com/" hreflang="en-us" />
<link rel="alternate" href="https://yourdomain.com/uk/" hreflang="en-gb" />
<link rel="alternate" href="https://yourdomain.com/ger/" hreflang="de-de" />
<link rel="alternate" href="https://yourdomain.com/" hreflang="de-ch" />
<link rel="alternate" href="https://yourdomain.com/che/" hreflang="fr-ch" />
<link rel="alternate" href="https://yourdomain.com/che/" hreflang="it-ch" />
<link rel="alternate" href="https://yourdomain.com/che/" hreflang="rm-ch" />
<link rel="alternate" href="https://yourdomain.com/" hreflang="x-default" />
```

Here's a breakdown of what each tag does:

- `link rel="alternate"` : This attribute indicates that the linked document is an alternate version of the current page.
- `href="URL"` : This specifies the URL of the alternate page.
- `hreflang="language-country"` : This attribute specifies the language and optional country/region of the target audience for that specific URL.

*Figure 5-16. Gemini hreflang output example*

You'll note that Gemini provides only one set of tags. This is because the same set of tags should be placed on each of the pages. Gemini explains in the key points section that each page also needs a self-referencing hreflang tag.

Once you have created the draft hreflang code and it's been verified by a developer, you can then push the code live on your site. Remember, you need to implement hreflang code for all the pages of your website that are duplicated in other languages and country-language variations. If you have a large or very large site, this can be very time-consuming, but generative AI makes the process go much faster!

## .htaccess Files

Generative AI tools can help write code for *.htaccess* files. These files are found on Apache web servers and can be very helpful in managing traffic on your website.

### .HTACCESS 301 REDIRECTS

You can use generative AI to implement redirects on your website. You might remove a folder and want to redirect to a different folder on your site, or you might want to redirect all *.asp* files to *.html* files (if you change your CMS, for example). Your prompt might look like Figure 5-17.

> Generate the .htaccess rewrite rules to 301-redirect pages per the following list:
>
> /articles to /content
> /blog to /content
> *.asp to *.html

*Figure 5-17. Example prompt for .htaccess 301 redirects*

In our example, we used ChatGPT-4o, and Figure 5-18 shows the response we received.

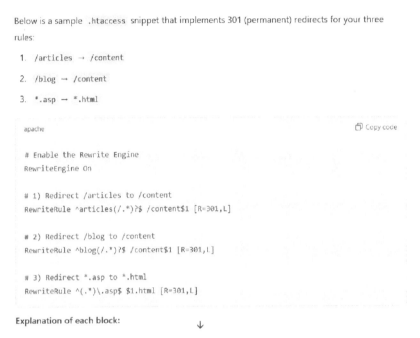

Below is a sample .htaccess snippet that implements 301 (permanent) redirects for your three rules:

1. /articles → /content

2. /blog → /content

3. *.asp → *.html

```apache
# Enable the Rewrite Engine
RewriteEngine On

# 1) Redirect /articles to /content
RewriteRule ^articles(/.*)?$ /content$1 [R=301,L]

# 2) Redirect /blog to /content
RewriteRule ^blog(/.*)?$ /content$1 [R=301,L]

# 3) Redirect *.asp to *.html
RewriteRule ^(.*)\.asp$ $1.html [R=301,L]
```

**Explanation of each block:**

*Figure 5-18. Example response for .htaccess 301 redirects*

Note that ChatGPT's *.htaccess* instructions include comments to explain what each directive is used for. It further explains each section, but we've trimmed the detailed explanation in Figure 5-18 for brevity.

Once you've reviewed the code, you'll need to add it to your *.htaccess* file and publish the modified file to your web server. Bear in mind that redirects in *.htaccess* files are hierarchical in nature, so where you put the code in the file can change its impact. Ensure that your developer is fully aware of these rules so that you can get your new code placed in the right location within the file. Then test it to make sure that the redirects are working properly and verify that you're not unintentionally redirecting other content.

## .HTACCESS BLOCK IP ADDRESS

Another good use for *.htaccess* files is to block IP addresses or IP address ranges from accessing your website. You might be wondering why you would want to do this, but there are times when it makes sense, such as:

- Blocking competing sites that are crawling your site
- Blocking user agents claiming to be Googlebot but that don't come from IP address ranges used by Googlebot
- Protecting your site against attacks (e.g., account takeovers or brute-force authentication)

*.htacess* files provide an efficient way to block IP addresses, and you can use generative AI to draft this code for you. Figure 5-19 shows a sample prompt you can use with your generative AI tool of choice.

Generate .htaccess rules to block access to domain.com from the following IP addresses:

999.999.999.045
888.888.888.*
777.888.999.*

*Figure 5-19. Example prompt for .htaccess block IP address*

Once again, we tried this with ChatGPT-4o, and Figure 5-20 shows the response we received.

As with *.htaccess* 301 redirects, your developer will need to review this code to ensure that it's properly structured. Then you should check your log files to verify that you're not blocking other crawlers you want to allow.

Below is a simple example of how you can block these IPs in .htaccess using Apache's access control directives. This snippet uses the older **Order/Deny/Allow** directives (often still supported on many servers). If your server uses the newer mod_authz_core syntax (Apache 2.4+), see the alternative example that follows.

## Older-Style (Apache < 2.4 or with `mod_authz_host`)

```apache
                                                                    Copy code
<IfModule mod_authz_host.c>
    Order Allow,Deny
    Deny from 999.999.999.045
    Deny from 888.888.888
    Deny from 777.888.999
    Allow from all
</IfModule>
```

### How it works

↓

- **Deny from 999.999.999.045** blocks exactly that IP.

*Figure 5-20. Example response for .htaccess block IP address*

## Conclusion

In this chapter, we've shown many ways that generative AI tools can make it easier to complete technical SEO tasks. This enables your team to reduce errors in their work and move onto more complex tasks, which is good for productivity and employee satisfaction.

In Chapter 6, we'll take the next step and start discussing more advanced ways that generative AI tools can scale your SEO program.

# PART III

# The Next Level of AI-Driven SEO

# 6

# Advanced Use Cases for Generative AI in SEO

With some technical skills or a developer team supporting you, you can create powerful customizations to use generative AI at scale to accelerate growth and increase revenues. Building SEO systems at scale is where you'll find the real power in generative AI. Instead of training junior SEO associates to research keyword targets or do competitive analysis, you can train a model and deploy it, which gives you an AI assistant at your fingertips with the ability to get your answers in seconds. Instead of scaling content creation by hiring additional writers, you can use generative AI to help your existing writers increase their output while improving their content quality.

We discussed the basics in Chapter 3, but in this chapter we'll look at the more technical side of scaling up with automation and generative AI. We'll dive deeper into generative AI implementation, including the infrastructure in retrieval-augmented generation (RAG), how to use enterprise APIs, and the benefits of generative AI for creating video and audio.

Automation for SEO practitioners increases productivity and reduces the time needed for many of your day-to-day tasks. This chapter covers the many benefits, use cases, and advantages of automation in SEO using generative AI. We'll also discuss customizing your own generative pretrained transformer (GPT).

## The Value of Using Generative AI at Scale

Think of generative AI as a team of junior associates that you can have do much of the tedious SEO legwork for you. Tasks they can perform on your behalf include:

- Discovering topics for your site that competitors don't cover
- Identifying areas of SEO weakness in your existing content that should be addressed
- Creating draft outlines for new content
- Researching key data points and sources for those data points that could add depth to your content
- Drafting sections of content for new articles on your site or even full articles

These are just some examples of how you might employ AI-based associates. You wouldn't expect to use the work they do without review by one of your expert staff, but their work makes your job of creating and improving your content much easier—and arguably increases the content's quality. The result is more cost-effective use of your time and effort.

Generative AI can effectively be your brainstorming and drafting partner, just as we described in the prior chapters, but on a larger scale if you have technical skills or access to developers. As we refer to ways to use generative AI in content development in this chapter (and throughout the book), this is how you should think about its value.

You can also improve the quality of the output of generative AI tools by connecting them to your own market-specific knowledge base, which will give you a competitive edge. Whatever your business, if you're not building your own knowledge base, you're going to fall behind. Your market knowledge base is a set of data points that AI can ingest to return an output of ideas, outlines, and summaries of your content, informed by your unique data. Data fuels AI and produces richer outputs and personalization from generative AI.

One prerequisite is some technical know-how. To take advantage of many of the advanced use cases mentioned in this chapter, you'll need some background knowledge in software engineering, or you'll need an engineering team to help with the technical aspects of the work. The technical investment will give you exponential returns, so it's worth the time and money necessary to invest in advanced generative AI use cases.

## AI-Powered SEO Tools for Inspiration

Before we get into the more advanced technical side of generative AI, we should mention that you can leverage several AI-powered features using premade tools already on the market with a long history of SEO benefits. These tools are much more limited than what you can do with your own programming and custom models, but they are a good starting point and can give you ideas for developing your own tools.

Let's say you want to find new content to publish on your site. You know you should focus on content that can get you more visibility, but where do you start looking for ideas? You could home in on trends, but how do you find these trends? Google Trends helps you get a general idea of topics, but it won't find you keywords to target. AI-powered tools can generate a long list of content topics to target based on keywords from third-party APIs, their popularity in users' search queries, and related keywords to suggest similar content you may not have thought about without the tools. The third-party APIs (e.g., Semrush or Ahrefs) require additional coding, but automation agents can use third-party APIs to come up with common keywords that you can then feed to generative AI models to find content topics and suggest titles.

In Chapter 4, we discussed manual processes for using generative AI for parts of this process; now envision AI agents querying these data sources and making the output better at scale, without manual intervention at each step. The main human intervention other than prompt tuning is the expert review and edits at the end.

AI-powered tools can also help with backlinking opportunities. Just like content topic ideas, you first need a third-party API to obtain information about competitors. Agents poll these APIs for competitor analysis and information, and then feed results to a generative AI model to find topics for backlinks or a gap analysis to understand your competitor's backlink profile better. You can use them to find where competitors have their backlinks or domains with similar keywords that might be beneficial. You can also discover mentions of your brand on social media or other sites with third-party APIs and use AI to analyze user feedback about your brand.

The following tools existed before GPTs and current generative AI models, but they each have their own AI that you can use in your agents and scripts:

*Semrush*

Semrush is a subscription service for keyword research, competitor analysis, and topic research for generative AI creation. It also has a rich database of your backlinks.

*Ahrefs*

Audit your backlink history and find opportunities for content topics. Ahrefs also can be used for keyword research.

*Grammarly*

Grammarly is beneficial for optimizing content and finding awkward wording to create more engaging content.

*Google Analytics*

Most SEO practitioners already work with Google Analytics, but it's a great tool for identifying traffic trends and optimizing ad content for better conversions.

*Yoast SEO*

The Premium version of Yoast SEO gives you AI-powered titles and meta descriptions. It also provides content suggestions for better search visibility.

## Custom GPTs for More Targeted Brand Content

In November 2023, OpenAI released functionality that enables users to create custom GPTs. Custom GPTs are beneficial for very defined use cases. When you build a custom GPT using an LLM like OpenAI's ChatGPT, you can use your own proprietary data, but ChatGPT will fall back on its knowledge base in scenarios when it does not have an answer from your data.

ChatGPT is great at helping you create content ideas, but you will want to narrow down topics to content related to your brand. For example, suppose you want to develop a chatbot to answer basic customer service questions. You don't need your chatbot lecturing users on the history of a product. You need the chatbot to provide information specific to the product that draws key information from your knowledge base. You can do this by creating your own custom GPT that focuses on just those topics.

Another good use for custom GPTs is to recommend products based on your users' search and purchase history—similar to the "people who bought this also bought" feature you see on many ecommerce sites. If you can save and store that data in a knowledge base, you can use a custom GPT to implement the solution. You can also use custom GPTs for content creation, language translations, and marketing messages created for social media (though these will still need human editors to check for accuracy and brand tone before publishing). Any generative AI product can be customized with its own GPT for your brand.

Before you create a custom GPT, you first need to define several factors:

- What do you want the GPT to generate? Answers to customers' questions? Content for your site?

- What tone do you want to use? Maybe you want to generate content in pirate-speak for children's learning or you want your GPT to stay professional and answer customers' queries. GPTs can generate responses using a specific tone and personality.

- What are your data sources? Will you be using a database of orders for your ecommerce chatbot assistant, recent search data collected from your site, or general knowledge about your market?

Answers to these questions will be used to set up and configure your custom GPT. Don't forget that you still need to monitor and continually update your GPT with new data as you incorporate more information in your knowledge base. After the GPT's initial deployment, it's common for businesses to find bugs or make changes to configurations as well.

## CREATING A CUSTOM GPT

To create a custom GPT, you first need an OpenAI Plus account. OpenAI has a free version of ChatGPT, but you cannot create custom GPTs or use the latest version of ChatGPT. As of the time of writing, a Plus subscription costs $20 per month. You can also work with a Team account for enterprises at $25 per person per month. The examples shared here were created using the Plus subscription of ChatGPT.

In your Plus OpenAI account, click the icon with your initials in the upper-right corner as shown in Figure 6-1 and then click My GPTs. OpenAI has its own tool to help you create your custom GPT, so you get some direction as you go through the process.

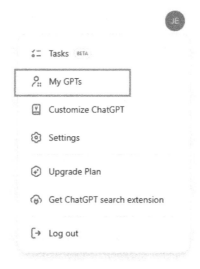

*Figure 6-1. OpenAI's drop-down menu for accessing custom GPTs*

Next, click Create a GPT, as shown in Figure 6-2.

## My GPTs

+ **Create a GPT**
Customize a version of ChatGPT for a specific purpose

*Figure 6-2. OpenAI interface to create a new custom GPT*

You're now in the interface to create your custom GPT. You should be looking at a web page like the one shown in Figure 6-3.

*Figure 6-3. First prompt to create a custom GPT in the OpenAI web interface*

Let's create a custom GPT that answers questions about writing a book. We want a GPT that helps writers understand the process of outlining, writing, editing, proofing, and publishing an ebook. Because ChatGPT is conversational, we can enter instructions using the same tone you would use to instruct a writer in person. We'll use the following prompt:

*I want a custom GPT that helps writers understand the process of outlining, writing, editing, proofing, and publishing an ebook.*

You'll see a wait message indicating that a custom GPT is being created. Then, you'll receive a suggestion for a GPT name. For simplicity, we'll use the suggested title "Ebook Guide" shown in the interface in Figure 6-4. ChatGPT will also generate a suggested image. For simplicity, we'll use the suggested image.

**Ebook Guide**
• Draft

Create                              Configure

visuals for new products" or "make a software engineer who helps format my code."

What would you like to make?

> I want a custom GPT that helps writers understand the process of
> outlining, writing, editing, proofing, and publishing an ebook

Great! Let's decide on a name for this GPT. How about **Ebook Guide**?

> Yes, use ebook guide as the GPT name.

Now, I'll generate an initial profile picture for **Ebook Guide**. Let's get started.

Here's the profile picture for **Ebook Guide**. Do you like it, or would you like any changes?

*Figure 6-4. OpenAI instructions for a custom GPT*

The example creates a custom GPT for you, but you can save yourself some time by using third-party custom GPTs available in the OpenAI marketplace. In the OpenAI interface, you'll see a button for Explore GPTs in the top-left corner. Clicking this button opens an interface where you can search for custom GPTs that others have developed. The quality and usefulness of these GPTs vary depending on the creators, but you can find dozens of custom GPTs for SEO already built and ready to use.

As an example, suppose you want to improve engagement with your content. Several custom GPTs are available that can help with content tweaks to improve readability and give the text a more human tone. You can also use these GPTs for keyword focusing, editing, fact-checking, analyzing content for gaps, analyzing links to compare your content with competitors' content, and numerous other tasks that you can leverage without the need to create and customize your own GPT.

## CONFIGURING YOUR GPT

At the top of the ChatGPT creation window is a Configure button. Click it to see the configuration options. For example, ChatGPT gives you suggested conversation starters to help your users, but you can write your own to fit your brand and the questions you commonly get from customers. In this window, you can also change the description and title of your GPT.

If you already have a knowledge base for your business, that's where the real power lies because you can generate content and answers for your brand and customers. In the configuration window, you can upload files to add your knowledge base to your custom GPT. Since this example is a chatbot to help writers, you could upload files with tips and tricks for outlining, writing chapters, and self-editing. This information is ingested and incorporated into your custom GPT's responses to queries.

For brands, you can upload files like data sheets or marketing brochures that explain your products. An enterprise could have thousands of pages of product information, and a custom GPT will ingest those in seconds and use the data for customer queries. Instead of training a team of people to answer questions, a custom GPT becomes your customer support team to help answer brand questions (though you will still want some level of human oversight).

Instructions for our custom GPT are shown in Figure 6-5.

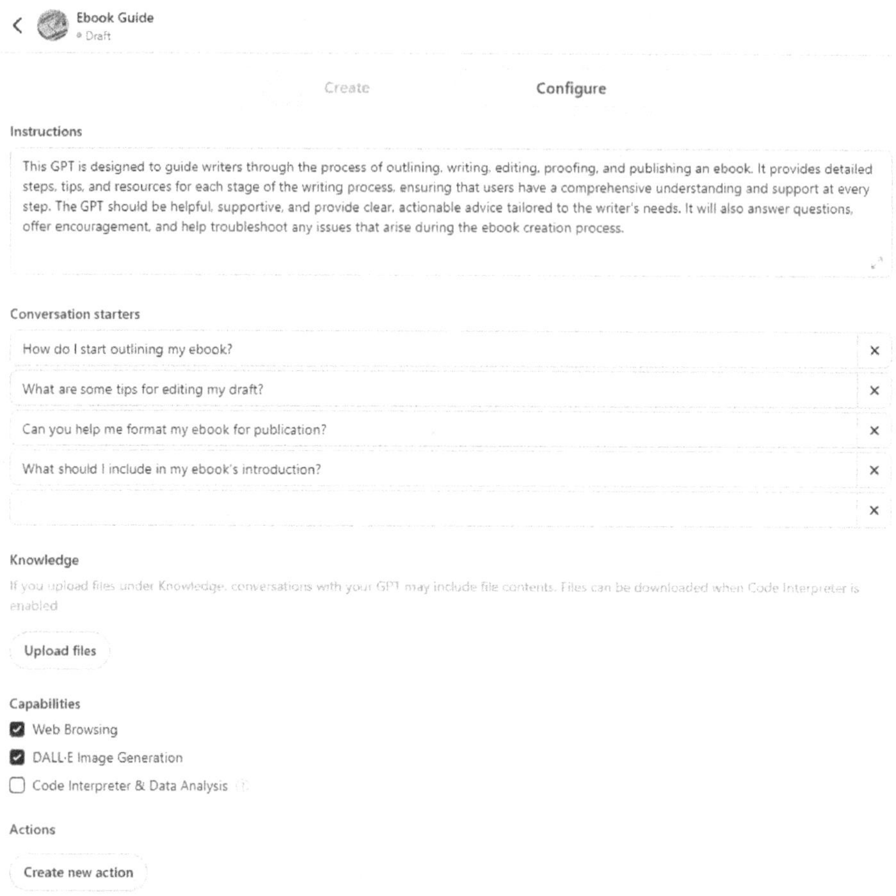

< **Ebook Guide**
  • Draft

Create                    Configure

**Instructions**

This GPT is designed to guide writers through the process of outlining, writing, editing, proofing, and publishing an ebook. It provides detailed steps, tips, and resources for each stage of the writing process, ensuring that users have a comprehensive understanding and support at every step. The GPT should be helpful, supportive, and provide clear, actionable advice tailored to the writer's needs. It will also answer questions, offer encouragement, and help troubleshoot any issues that arise during the ebook creation process.

**Conversation starters**

| How do I start outlining my ebook? | × |

| What are some tips for editing my draft? | × |

| Can you help me format my ebook for publication? | × |

| What should I include in my ebook's introduction? | × |

| | × |

**Knowledge**

If you upload files under Knowledge, conversations with your GPT may include file contents. Files can be downloaded when Code Interpreter is enabled.

Upload files

**Capabilities**
☑ Web Browsing
☑ DALL·E Image Generation
☐ Code Interpreter & Data Analysis

**Actions**

Create new action

*Figure 6-5. Configuration window for a custom GPT*

Notice that you can give your custom GPT image generation capabilities. You could include this option if you want to create custom images for your brand. For basic chatbots, you probably don't want to allow this option. Another added function is code interpretation. You might use this function, for example, if you have a custom GPT for a GitHub library where the GPT can answer questions about coding errors and bugs.

You can also hook your custom GPT into external APIs. The external APIs can feed your custom GPT's data and knowledge. For example, suppose you want to continually feed new data to a user's web shopping interface in an ecommerce store. You can feed data from an API to the custom GPT in real time to constantly update a customer's suggestions with seasonal or current news content with an abnormal spike in popularity.

In addition, you can create GPT actions, which enable users of your custom GPTs to make calls to APIs of tools outside ChatGPT so that you can significantly extend the functionality of your GPT. Users continue to make their requests using natural language, and the GPT automatically converts those requests into the JSON schema required by the API. This can include accessing third-party data stores, so you don't need to download copies of their data, and it increases the resiliency of your custom GPT by allowing it to always access the latest data rather than a potentially outdated data store that you may have downloaded.

After you're finished configuring your GPT, click Create in the upper-right corner. You can publish it to only yourself (the "Only me" option), to anyone with the link (such as sharing with a team), or to the GPT store. The GPT store makes your custom GPT available to the public.

After you create a custom GPT, your job isn't over, though. You still need to test it. Your custom GPT will be available in your OpenAI dashboard. After publishing the GPT, you can click on it and ask it questions.

As with anything AI, you never want to "set it and forget it" without any review, especially if you use advanced configurations with API integration. You might need to change the knowledge section or tweak the data returned by your API. Even after you tweak the custom GPT, you should check it thoroughly to ensure that it's still returning helpful answers to customers' queries.

## Personalized and Dynamic Content Optimization

The power of generative AI is in its ability to generate personalized and dynamic content at scale. The "at scale" power of generative AI is in automation.

We created a custom GPT in the previous section, so now we'll talk about generating personalized and dynamic content. GPT is sufficient for basic queries, but more advanced automation is done with a system called *retrieval-augmented generation* (RAG). RAG feeds data into an LLM from various sources that you control, ensuring that the generative AI tool you're working with uses information that you know is correct. For RAG, you need more technical skills, but you can completely automate many of the manual SEO procedures that you might currently perform.

### AN INTRODUCTION TO RAG

RAG architecture incorporates LLMs with traditional data storage systems. For example, you can use RAG with a standard relational database collecting data from a custom GPT, or you can use it with large datasets collected from web searches or knowledge bases. SEO practitioners can use RAG for generating content from data collected in keyword research, backlink analysis, or locally from your brand's site.

Merging data retrieval with dynamic data enables RAG systems to find similarity in content and use your unique knowledge base in crafting the output. LLMs take time to train, and many common models work with slightly older data, so they aren't aware of more recent events. You can make the more recent information available through your RAG system. More important, using custom data will be much more efficient than relying on the data from broad LLM systems, and it can more easily be personalized for highly dynamic businesses. RAG architecture lets LLMs retrieve data during the time it takes to process a user query, allowing LLMs to ingest data in real time to produce more accurate answers with as much relevant context as possible. You get higher generative AI accuracy with content generation at scale. You can still get errors once you implement RAG to address them, but you can reduce the rate at which they occur.

An LLM needs data to provide accurate answers, and generative AI tools still have significant issues with accuracy when data is insufficient. For example, suppose you want to identify common questions from a chatbot. Your chatbot collects questions and stores them in a relational database. You can feed an LLM questions and answers from the relational database to then generate content and upload it to a WordPress blog hosting your knowledge base. This process can be used to protect you from hallucinations that the generative AI tool may make. The term *hallucinations* describes the inaccurate results you might get from AI when the LLM does not have enough reference material or simply references incorrect information found online.

RAG content generation provides a personalized experience for your readers. Your business might launch a new product, so you now need to generate content for a knowledge base. It can take weeks to build out a large knowledge base for a new product, but generative AI can provide you with a draft for human review in minutes. APIs can have hundreds of endpoints, but generative AI can generate draft developer knowledge base content in minutes when developers deploy their solution. Anytime you need personalized content based on custom brand input, generative AI can help.

## THE MANY DIFFERENT TYPES OF LLMS

Before you build out your RAG architecture, you need to determine which LLM you want to use. You have several options, but each one has its own tone when it writes content. For example, ChatGPT is one of the most popular generative AI models available, but it can be much more robotic sounding and verbose than some of the other platforms. Claude, on the other hand, produces content that is considered much closer to sounding human.

### Note

AI is quickly evolving, so it's important to note that new LLMs and updates to existing LLMs will be available after the publication of this book. It's likely that newer versions are available as you're reading this.

Here are a few LLMs as of May 2025 that you can consider working with:

*ChatGPT-4.5 and OpenAI o1*

ChatGPT-4.5 is one of the more popular and flexible multimodal LLMs. It also has DALL-E for creating images. It's fast and has been trained on the billions of pages published on the internet, including trillions of words of text, code, and translations. OpenAI fine-tunes its LLM with reinforcement learning from human feedback (RLHF), which you can use to improve results as you work with the model. OpenAI o1 integrates advanced reasoning and is better for advanced coding, scientific research, or anything that requires step-by-step problem-solving. Keep in mind that o1 is slower and costs more per token. (*Tokens* are like credits or digital currency to "pay" for generative AI output.)

*Anthropic Claude 3.7 Sonnet and Opus*

As of this writing, Claude 3.7 Sonnet is the most recent LLM model from Anthropic. It's known for having more humanlike output, but it also excels at analyzing visual input, such as graphs or photos. Sonnet is best for multistep workflows and is particularly effective for orchestrating tasks that require fast processing and context-sensitive responses. Claude Opus performs well with advanced content creation. It's known for its ability to handle intricate tasks like generating detailed research reports, analyzing complex data, and creating high-quality content that demands a deeper understanding.

*Google Gemini 1.5 Pro and 1.5 Flash*

Google has been using AI for years and published the original paper on transformers—the technology that LLMs are based on—in 2017. As of this writing, Google has two notable models: Google Gemini 1.5 Pro and 1.5 Flash. Both AI models can process text, images, audio, and video, but they have different uses and are optimized for different tasks. Gemini 1.5 Pro is designed for complex tasks and is better for deep reasoning and nuanced understanding. It can perform sophisticated reasoning tasks, such as generating summaries of long-form text, audio recordings, or video content. Gemini 1.5 Pro can also be used for content creation, story writing, and scriptwriting. Gemini 1.5 Flash is optimized for rapid response times and is better for applications that require quick processing and low latency. It's ideal for time-sensitive tasks, such as chat applications and real-time data analytics.

*Google PaLM 2*

PaLM 2 is designed for language applications while Gemini is designed for multimodal applications. PaLM 2 is better at advanced tasks like summarization and question answering in languages it knows well. Gemini is better at creative writing, such as poems, lyrics, or dialogue. If you're dealing only with text-based modalities and need translations, you might consider PaLM 2 (*https://oreil.ly/yqCV4*) to help produce content at scale for multiple languages.

Several open source models also exist if you want to lower costs and customize models. We'll discuss why and when to use custom LLMs in "Building RAG Architecture" on page 171, but know that you have several options for open source LLMs if you have the technical expertise (or technical team) to customize a preexisting model. Open source LLMs may require a steeper learning curve but could have a lower overall cost of ownership after setup. Open source models are available to anyone, so vulnerabilities must be reported to the creator to be patched. Vulnerabilities are dangerous because they can be used to poison results or gain access to your data.

A few of the available open source models include:

*Milvus*
A vector database built for scale and machine learning applications

*Meta Llama*
An AI model provided for text-based output

*Grok*
An AI model for text-based output but built to be more conversational

## BUILDING RAG ARCHITECTURE

The algorithms and backend processing for RAG are complex, but creating the architecture has only two steps:

1. User input, such as a query from your site's search functionality or a chatbot question

2. The source data, which could be a database, a group of dynamically created files, a NoSQL database, web pages, or any other source that can be fed to an LLM

Although creating a custom GPT requires no coding, creating RAG architecture requires some technical knowledge. You can use your own local LLMs with RAG. We'll use the same custom GPT that we created previously to generate output content. You can see an example of RAG infrastructure in Figure 6-6.

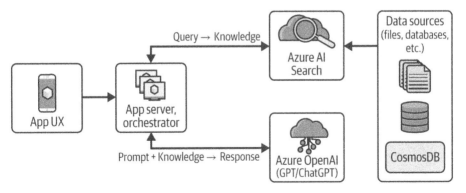

*Figure 6-6. General overview of RAG infrastructure*

Suppose you need to create content about your brand, but you don't want it to include knowledge that is too general about your products. Your brand might sell mobile phone accessories, but you don't want a history of mobile phones in your content collection. You can use your own brand content to feed an LLM—in this case, ChatGPT—and then build content based on the input.

In the following example, we'll use keyword input to build brand content from a corpus of web pages on your site. For example, suppose you did some keyword research (which, incidentally, can be automated with AI, but more on that later), and you want to use common search phrases to build content around your brand. You can automate this using your language of choice. Examples in this section will use Python.

To create a RAG implementation, you need three things:

- A corpus, or the collection of data the LLM will use to generate content

- The API for ChatGPT for the LLM

- Content generation from input of keywords or search phrases

## Gathering the corpus

The first step to creating a RAG implementation is to gather the corpus. The *corpus* is the collection of data used to train AI. It's a fancy term for "background knowledge." You can use any amount of corpus data, including information stored in a database, web pages, static files, and even images.

Without the corpus, you will get general information in response to the input provided. For example, if you input "mobile phone," you'll get all kinds of output ranging from the history of the mobile phone to mobile phone vendors to questions and answers about fixing a mobile phone. If you're selling accessories, this information will pollute your content output. The corpus will train the LLM on your brand and target audience so that you can get much more precise and accurate results.

In our example, a local collection of brand web pages will serve as the corpus. In a real-world situation, you'd crawl your site or use a sitemap to add to the corpus, but for simplicity we'll use hardcoded text for our example. The following code example has a sentence or two to represent a brand page, but your web pages will contain several lines of content to train the LLM. Notice that the corpus is specific to our brand:

```
brand_corpus = [
    "This yellow mobile phone case is perfect for the iPhone 16 and can...",
    "Mobile phone cases are perfect for protecting your device from rain...",
    "Our mobile phone accessories cost between $10 and $100 and can be..."
]
```

## Connecting to the LLM API

After you have the corpus, you then need to connect to the LLM API. For this example, we'll use ChatGPT as the LLM, but several others have APIs (e.g., Microsoft Azure, Google Cloud, Anthropic, Hugging Face). You'll need an account, which must be a paid account for any of the major LLMs. Every API also requires access keys. You can find out how to generate keys for your account in the LLM's documentation. We'll assume you have the OpenAI Python library installed. If not, you can use the following install prompt in your Python development interface:

```
pip install --upgrade openai
```

With OpenAI installed, you can now create a connection to the ChatGPT API:

```
from openai import OpenAI
client = OpenAI(api_key="...")
```

## Generating content from user input

Now you need the code to pull a document—a web page in this scenario—and you'll work with user input to create content. Our user input is from keyword research. Keyword research can be done manually using the SEO tools mentioned in "AI-Powered SEO Tools for Inspiration" on page 159, or you can perform research using automated agents (discussed in the next section). For this example, it's assumed you have a list of keywords in a text file:

```
from openai import OpenAI
client = OpenAI(api_key="your_api_key")

brand_corpus = [
    "This yellow mobile phone case is perfect for the iPhone 16 and can...",
    "Mobile phone cases are perfect for protecting your device from rain...",
    "Our mobile phone accessories cost between $10 and $100 and can be..."
]
```

```
prompt = (
  "Create a 500 word article and incorporate brand information "
  "from this content: {brand_page}. Use this keyword as the "
  "focus for the topic: {keyword}."
)

response = client.chat.completions.create(
  model="gpt-4",
  messages=[
    {
      "role": "user",
      "content": prompt.format(
          brand_page=brand_content[0],
          keyword="iphone 16"
      )
    }
  ]
)

print(response)
```

This example is simple, but you can incorporate agent output and automation into content generation and RAG. The important part of this code is the prompt. The prompt is sent to the LLM and tells it what to use to generate content.

LLMs can generate more than simple page content. You could use competitor analysis to create a list of publications for backlink opportunities, find the top five competitor pages and their keywords to create drafts of your own content, create outlines from a gap analysis from your pages compared to competitors' pages, or simply make content based on trending keywords, just like we did here.

Using RAG gives your brand the ability to work with real-time data for content generation, but you don't always need human queries. You can automate draft content generation using agents to identify keywords and input these keywords into your RAG system.

## Custom LLMs or building from scratch

In the preceding example, we used ChatGPT as the model, but you aren't limited to common LLMs. You can also use custom LLMs, but you should use them only with very specific use cases. The common LLMs mentioned previously have trillions of data points to work with, so you can ask them anything with varying degrees of results. With a custom LLM, you define the model and limit it to your specific use case. For most businesses, a custom LLM is not necessary. The model will be able to produce results only on certain data, so it does not have the additional information available with common LLMs.

To create your own LLM, you need the infrastructure, a large corpus, testing resources, technical development experience, and funds to host it. Models require graphics processing unit (GPU) hours to compute training. You can use cloud providers to train a model, but of course you must pay for the resources. It costs about $1–$2 per GPU hour, so a small 10-billion parameter model that takes about 100,000 GPU hours could cost you up to $200,000 to train. For a frame of reference, Llama 2 has about 70 billion parameters, so it can cost well over $1 million to train a large model.

There are four steps in building an LLM from scratch:

*Curating the data*
> This is the most time-consuming step. You need accurate, quality, deduplicated data and a source with enough information to train the model. You can use the internet, but you can also use public datasets, including Common Crawl and Hugging Face. Another option is using an LLM to create a dataset. Datasets should be diverse, depending on your desired output. You can use web pages, code, books, news, articles, and scientific journals.

*Building the model architecture*
> This is a neural network with attention mechanisms to match input with output. Neural networks identify patterns and context so that a word can be "understood" compared to other similar words. For example, the neural network must identify the position and sequence of a word like *park*. It must identify if the word means to park a vehicle or a public place where people hang out.

*Training*
> Training at scale is complex and requires high-value GPUs, mentioned previously.

*Testing and review*
> You must evaluate and review the results of your model. The Hugging Face site has benchmarks that can be used to identify the success of your model.

As you can tell, building your own LLM requires extreme technical knowledge. You need a team to help you and a large budget for compute power. If your use case is very specific, you can generate content that is highly targeted and effective at selling your brand services. This can boost sales and make it easier to build thousands of pages for your business with a good return on your investment, but it's a long-term, high-value project that must be carefully planned first.

## AUTOMATING SEO TASKS WITH AI

Think of AI agents as your automated assistants. Your automated SEO assistant might know that every morning you need keyword research on the latest trends affecting your brand. The agent pulls information from an API and inputs keywords into generative AI prompts for content suggestions. An AI agent can gather this data for you every day, so you don't have to rely on a person to perform this task. Your AI agent can also analyze trends multiple times during the day so that you can change your goals as trends change, making your marketing much more effective.

Suppose that after an agent performs trend analysis for you, you decide to create content or perform competitor analysis to see if competitors are ranking for specific keywords already. You can have multiple agents "talking" to one another to make decisions based on their own output. The AI agent gathering trends every morning can send output to another agent that will make the decision to generate content based on competitor analysis. The second agent can take these trends, find the top five pages for related search terms, and decide if content should be generated. Content generation decisions can also be sent to a third agent to create draft content ideas based on its own analysis.

Agents are powerful automation tools, but they need a goal. When you build an agent, you can integrate generative AI models to help agents make decisions. For example, you can have an agent using Claude to evaluate content generated from ChatGPT. The back-and-forth evaluation can be used to generate and evaluate content until you create a piece that fits your tone and brand style.

In this section, we'll break down the components of an agent system for generating content for a brand.

### Infrastructure for AI agents

An AI agent is like a script running silently on a machine. Figure 6-7 shows a few potential roles for agents.

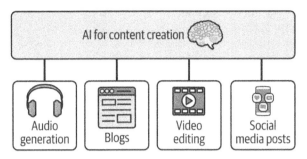

*Figure 6-7. Potential roles for agents*

When you build your own agents, you need infrastructure to host them. The development can be done in any language, but AI is generally built with Python because of its prebuilt libraries, which are freely available to developers. You aren't limited to Python, though, and some businesses choose to use R, Java, C++, JavaScript, Lisp, and other languages.

You'll likely use hosting in the cloud for the ease of resource allocation, but you need more than host machines. Here are several factors to consider for your AI agent infrastructure:

*Database storage and management*
>AI requires data for training, and your database of choice can store it. You don't need a database if you plan to ingest data entirely from the internet, but chances are you will want to log errors and track what your AI agent is doing, which still requires a database to store this data. Also consider the type of data you plan to store. Unstructured data requires a NoSQL database, but structured data can use traditional relational databases. For example, storing web page data is easier with unstructured databases like MongoDB, but logged events could use a relational database like MariaDB or PostgreSQL.

*Internet access*
>Your agents will likely run on a local network, but they need access to the internet if you plan to understand the third-party content on your topic out there, use third-party APIs, or post content to your public-facing site.

*Virtual machines or compute resources*
>Agents are like services that execute an action at a time you program. This could be once a day or multiple times a day. You need a host machine and compute resources to run the agent and process its results. Don't provision

resources that handle only the initial agent processing. You want enough resources for scaling as you acquire more data and add more agent tasks.

*Security*

Don't forget that security should be integrated into your design workflow. Poor security could open your business to lawsuits or data disclosure. Validate data, especially when using external internet sources for ingestion and output.

## Agent roles

We will have four agents that will fulfill the following roles:

*SEO analyst*

This agent will take common keywords for a brand and get the top articles (or top list of articles) from competitors ranking for them.

*Researcher*

You want content that can perform better than a competitor, so the researcher will evaluate each section of content.

*Writer*

The research agent will feed output to the writer agent, and this agent will generate ideas and—if necessary—a summary of these ideas used for drafting content with generative AI. A human writer can then take these ideas and write content that will be fed to the content editor. You might even have a human editor review content and skip the content editor agent.

*Content editor*

The first pass on draft content might not match what you need, so an editor agent can be used to identify mismatched tone and technical information.

**SEO analyst.**    As an SEO practitioner, you likely monitor specific keywords for your brand. You might have a list of trending keywords, a list of seasonal keywords, and general brand-related keywords used to generate content. You could manually identify competitor performance in search engines, but an AI-powered agent can do it for you. An agent will take less time to perform this step, and it can perform analysis several times a day rather than having to rely on an analyst to do this manually. You might even automate this step, having this agent feed into the next agent to increase efficiency.

The SEO analyst agent can pull the top list of articles either from a third-party API or using your own search engine scraping solution. Not only will the agent identify the top-ranking pages, but it will also extract the content from each article. Every agent needs a goal, and this agent's goal is to pull top-ranking articles for a list of keywords. As you can imagine, this is a full-time job for a human SEO analyst, but AI-powered agents can perform this activity in seconds. An SEO analyst agent is your first step to using AI to power activity at scale without staffing limitations.

As you build this agent, you write code to cover the actions that other agents need to perform. Here are a few examples of tasks you might need agents to do, all of which can be prompts entered into one of the common models:

- Keep a log of sites you want to track, such as competitors' sites or sites that have content you want to analyze. Make sure to create prompts with a list of sites or ask the model to pull a list of the top-ranking content for a specific search query.

- Extract content from code. This can be done using a third-party library. You need headers, title, and section content, but you don't need code or formatting. You should keep links, though, and their anchor text.

- Avoid recrawling the same content over and over. Some server headers return a last updated variable, but that's rare. It might be worth keeping a log of URLs previously scraped unless you want to analyze updated content. To save resources, you can recrawl competitor content only when the search ranking increases.

- Server statistics might be useful if you are analyzing redirects or errors, so it may be helpful to pull and log server responses. For example, the first time you pull articles could result in a server 404 error, so you want to retry when the agent performs its activity again.

**Researcher.** After you extract content from top-ranking search links, you need to analyze the content. The SEO analyst agent sends its output to the researcher agent. At scale, this is where the power of AI can really make you more efficient. A person could feasibly go through several articles during the day to identify content quality, but they can't go through dozens of articles a day without help. The SEO research agent uses an LLM to analyze the content for opportunities to improve.

As the researcher analyzes content, it must determine content keywords and if your brand has opportunities to write better content. It's important to note that you want better content, not content that's "just as good." The SEO researcher agent can help perform this step for you in seconds. With an objective analysis, the next agent can assist with building draft content.

To generate better content, the researcher agent might even perform secondary searches based on extracted keywords or work with your current brand content to identify whether content should be added to existing articles rather than creating an entirely new page. You might have a page already ranking in search engines, so you may choose to add new relevant content to that. The researcher agent could also do a gap analysis to identify the difference between competitors' content and your own so that you can improve your content in line with what's ranking in search.

The researcher agent is limited only by what you can code. You can have additional researcher agents in your scaled system, but for this example, we'll use the goal of identifying additional content that can be generated on your site. After the researcher agent has finished its analysis, new content ideas are sent to the writer agent.

Much of the "meat" of your analysis can be done with this agent. Here are a few technical aspects that should be coded into your agent:

- Extract keywords using generative AI prompts for help. You could code your own extractor, but that would be extremely tedious. Generative AI can do this for you.

- Compare the title of the article with your own and other articles ranking in search engines. Research agents can suggest better titles to potentially improve rankings.

- Perform a gap analysis on your content with the content extracted from top-ranking articles. You can prompt generative AI to do the gap analysis for you, so you don't need to create any complex code that could take days to build and test.

- Using a gap analysis and generative AI results, determine the content you want to write and the content you want to update. You might have content that must be rewritten or sections that need to be added. Other keywords could be used to generate new content.

- Use a secondary model to fact-check content.

**Writer.** If you already use an LLM to write draft content, you know the prompts involved with writing. The writer agent calls an LLM API to draft the content. You'll need to experiment to find the LLM that works best for you. Most people think of ChatGPT for content creation, but ChatGPT's output can often seem robotic. You can still use ChatGPT if that's your preference. Your reviews and the editor agent (discussed in the next section) should perform fact-checking and validate content tone.

The prompt you use for the LLM depends on your goals. This agent sends the writing prompt to the LLM's API. You'll need the keyword, tone, intent (e.g., informational or transactional), audience, and any brand pages you want to use to shape the draft content around your own products. The API returns content, but you can't leave generative AI to write content without any type of validation.

As you build your agent system, always review the content to ensure it is still accurate and that the agents are working as they should. When LLMs deploy version upgrades, you may want to upgrade your generative AI draft content process for the latest version. An update will generate different content compared to older versions, so always review new content after upgrading the version.

The writer agent is familiar territory if you've already used generative AI for content. The difference is that the agent automates the creation of draft content. Some technical tasks of this agent include:

- Generate section headers to separate content and make it easier for users to scan and find the information they want to read.

- Ask generative AI to create engaging call-to-action links to your products.

- Include links to other content within your site.

- Generate meta descriptions, titles, and a summary of the content.

- Build questions and answers and focus content on problems that your brand solves.

- Use examples of your own content or content that you like to get the style and tone you're looking for.

Note the emphasis on draft content creation in this section. Generative AI cannot be depended upon to write content that you can publish without expert human review. Recall our analogy of having a team of junior researchers working for you from earlier in this chapter. Generative AI is prone to mistakes, it will miss important things, it will not capture your position accurately, and more. The editor agent that we discuss in the next section helps make your content better by addressing some of these issues, but you still need expert human review before you publish.

**Editor.** The final agent in your system checks the writer agent's draft content. Just as in a real-world publishing system, a writer needs an editor to identify awkward wording, factual issues, or unclear sections or to add content that improves the quality and readability of the text. The editor agent performs this step without you having to hire dozens of editors. With generative AI, you create content at a greater scale than you can with human writers, so you need to scale your editors as well.

As mentioned in the previous section, you should have a second LLM check for errors and content tone instead of the same one. This will improve the accuracy of the results. If the editor agent has issues with content, you could send it back to the writer agent to have the content rewritten. Another option is having the editor generate improved content, but this depends on your system design. How you set up your agent design depends on your preferences, but we recommend having your editor agent validate content only and send feedback to the writer agent. This keeps your system compartmentalized so that you can easily make changes to content generation in one location.

The editor agent can also log feedback and content-generation events for further review to help you with your management. For example, you may want to know how much content was kicked back to the writer agent for factual mistakes, which is serious when you want to be seen as an authority in your industry. The editor agent can log these events so that you can take a look when too many mistakes are being made. You might need to tweak the prompt, or your code could have logic errors.

As with human writers, the draft content output from generative AI needs an editor. You need to fact-check output and ensure that the content has a human tone. Some models like ChatGPT can sound very robotic, but other models, such as Claude, are known for sounding a bit more humanlike, so check for the tone of the output.

Here are a few technical points for creating an editor agent:

- Fact-check output. You fact-checked competitor content with the researcher agent, but you must again fact-check the new output to avoid publishing embarrassing misinformation on your brand site.

- Check for tone using a third model. For example, use Claude to check ChatGPT content for any tone issues or errors.

- Send content to a human reviewer before publishing any AI-generated content.
- If any errors are found, this agent can send content back to a writer agent to reanalyze and re-create it.

## Using Enterprise Platforms for Large-Scale Projects

As we have said before, the power of advanced generative AI is in its ability to scale your SEO projects. You can easily generate one or two articles a day for your site, but AI can help you increase content production while improving content quality. In Chapter 2, we mentioned that using AI for content can increase throughput by 30%, reduce costs by 30%, and increase quality by 30%.

To scale at an enterprise level, you need enterprise platforms. Several cloud platforms offer APIs and computing resources to support massive agent systems, generative AI content generation, automated analysis, and any other code-based SEO project. If you can code it, you need a place to host it.

The biggest and most popular platforms are:

*Microsoft Azure*
> Microsoft has made a large investment in OpenAI and is the creator of Copilot. OpenAI's API (*https://oreil.ly/dtTcC*) has endpoints for chatbots, content management, and direct questions and answers.

*Amazon Web Services (AWS)*
> Amazon has several APIs and endpoints for all types of machine learning and generative AI. For example, Amazon Bedrock (*https://oreil.ly/e98mO*) helps with building generative AI applications. Bedrock can also be used in RAG.

*OpenAI*
> OpenAI has a convenient API for content generation (*https://oreil.ly/jgFL7*). ChatGPT is popular for content generation, so it's likely you'll have at least one agent using the API.

*Google Cloud Platform (GCP)*
> Google has an agent builder (*https://oreil.ly/6j69Z*) that you can use to alleviate much of the technical overhead of building your own infrastructure. Vertex Agent Builder API can help with your workflows, and Gemini is beneficial for generating text and images.

You aren't limited to these four platforms, but these have integrated AI APIs and services already available. If you choose a smaller provider, make sure they have the resources to support generative AI and AI-powered automation.

### Tip

Once you integrate with a single API provider, you are tied to that particular provider. Therefore, you should ensure that the provider has all the features and scalability options for your current and future SEO projects.

Any API that you choose will be integrated into your agent programming. It does the heavy lifting for you so that you can rely on the third-party infrastructure to assist with generating content. The writing agent from our AI agent system example could use one of the content generation APIs to build the content, for example.

Before you adopt a specific model, you must understand its limitations and what you can do to scale your operations. Using enterprise platforms is about scaling, but not every API offers the speed and content quality you need. The following are some of the most important features you'll want to consider when selecting a provider for large-scale projects:

*Availability*

Most large providers offer at least 99% uptime service-level agreements, but regions are important for enterprise-level processing. The farther a region is from your processing, the more latency you'll experience with a delay in transferring data. Availability regions are data centers present in the general geographic location of your business and your users. To take it a step further, availability zones are located in regions of a site user's country for redundancy. For example, Azure has 54 regions in 140 countries, AWS has 66 availability zones, and GCP has 173 zones (*https:// oreil.ly/wnDB8*). Should one data center suffer from an outage, another availability zone can take over. Redundancy is important for failover and uptime.

*Latency*

Latency is the time it takes for data to transfer over the network, including processing at the database. Having low latency is critical to your application's performance. CPU and storage performance play a part in latency, and these factors can turn a one-hour process into a daylong one if they are not optimized. When you have to use more computing to reduce latency, you will likely incur higher costs. Optimizing computing resources is a must and requires the technical know-how to create a scalable infrastructure that doesn't waste your budget.

Every provider does well with offering computing and networking power for various data-transfer sizes. Benchmarks (*https://oreil.ly/jUA1t*) show that GCP does the best with processing power, AWS does the best with network throughput, and Azure does the best with I/O throughput. You can test your applications on all three, but fast computing power and network performance are most important when working with large data searches and AI processing.

*Cost*

The cost of your applications will vary depending on the billing model you choose and the amount of resources you use. All providers have tools that help you estimate how much you will spend each month based on the resources you deploy, but your costs will also depend on the number of resources used during agent deployments and processing and the number of times you call the provider's APIs. If you're not careful, you can get blindsided by high costs when your applications make too many resource calls. These resource calls could be deliberate, or you could have logic errors that exhaust your budget.

All three providers offer on-demand payment plans, but they have alternatives for enterprise pricing that give discounts for high-resource applications. As of this writing, Azure has a plan named ExpressRoute for leasing a private cloud, meaning your data never leaves the data center. This option is great for businesses with strict compliance requirements.

Depending on your resources and data usage, you could pay from a couple of hundred dollars a month to a few thousand. It's difficult to say exactly how much you will pay, so check the provider's calculator to help you estimate.

*API quotas and token limits*

API quotas and costs could be considered the same, but providers often have subscription requirements or limitations to the number of API requests. Limitations are set to avoid a denial-of-service (DoS) attack on the API servers but are usually based on your subscription model. Any calls over the limitations could be extremely costly.

The cost of accidentally making too many calls to an API with quotas isn't just a few hundred dollars. Going over API quotas can cost you tens of thousands of dollars. Mistakes happen when you have a subscription with high charges after you go over a certain number of requests or you have logic errors in your code. Let's say you have a logic error that turns what you think is 5 requests into 50 requests. Your code runs several times an hour. You could then have hundreds of unforeseen requests to an API. If you don't plan for these requests, you could get an unpleasant surprise when you receive the cloud provider's bill.

Each model and API have different token limits and context-window limitations as well. The impact will depend on your use case.

## Building Your Own AI Tools and Plug-ins

By now, you should be familiar with the typical prompt interfaces provided by model vendors, but you can also use APIs to build enterprise-tier plug-ins and tools. As an example, let's say you have a team of marketing people responsible for generating content. You might have Microsoft Teams set up for them to speak throughout the day. You can create bots for Teams (and other collaboration software), so you could create a bot in Teams where all your marketing people can generate content.

A Teams bot acts like a user added to your Teams group. A custom bot can give an array of different replies to user messages, and a generative AI bot can provide content ideas for your marketing team. The bot looks like a standard user account. If you're familiar with Slack, you know that a bot instantly greets you when you join a new server. It looks and acts like a real user, but you send it specific commands to ask how to use Slack. The same can be done with a Teams bot, except this bot will take prompts and instructions from your marketing team and provide output text that can be used for content.

Let's use a simple example of writing content about US presidents. You know from "Automating SEO Tasks with AI" on page 176 that you can use code to analyze a web page, but we want assistance with generating content about the US president James Polk at scale. ChatGPT will let you use an example to shape the way it outputs content, so you don't even need your own analysis code. ChatGPT will do it for you. As shown in Figure 6-8, the Biden White House archive provides information about Polk, so our bot will be instructed to take information from this page and generate content ideas.

*Figure 6-8. Biden White House archive page on President Polk*

A Teams bot can be coded in any language, but we will use Python in this example. In the earlier agents system example, we used Python to create a small application that pulled answers from ChatGPT. Instead of prompting ChatGPT to answer a question, our Teams bot will generate draft content for anyone in marketing (or another department) who sends it a message with specific prompts. The Python code can interface with the generative AI model—in our example, it's ChatGPT—and send back content. The advantage is that you could have 20 marketing people generating draft content and ideas from one location, and they can collaboratively determine strategies for SEO. For example, suppose you have a site selling computer equipment. NVIDIA announces a new GPU, so you need to generate content to keep up with the trend and help drive traffic to your local site. Your marketing team can chat with a Teams bot to come up with ideas and draft pages to publish during the spike in interest for new NVIDIA GPUs.

We'll keep our example simple by focusing on content from the White House page on Polk. ChatGPT has plenty of content and information to generate good content on old topics, but you still need to review output. A human reviewer can identify errors or low-quality content, so always have a gatekeeper review output before it's published to your site. The Teams interface lets you install your own bot from the Apps interface. Coding a full bot is beyond the scope of the book, but after you code a bot, you must upload the code from your Teams interface. You also need privileges to make bots available in Teams, so check with your Teams administrator if you do not have permission.

Our bot connects to the ChatGPT API, and we can ask it to write content with the White House web page as a reference, as shown in Figure 6-9.

*Figure 6-9. Example request for a Teams bot named StudyAI*

As you can see, we ask the Teams chatbot to write us content based on the White House URL. The chatbot takes a minute and responds with what's shown in Figure 6-10.

**James K. Polk: The Dark Horse President**

James Knox Polk, the 11th President of the United States, served from 1845 to 1849. His presidency, though short, was marked by significant expansion and strong leadership. Known as the "dark horse" candidate for his unexpected nomination by the Democratic Party, Polk's tenure in office was instrumental in shaping the nation's boundaries and its destiny.

Born on November 2, 1795, in Mecklenburg County, North Carolina, Polk was a diligent student with a passion for law and politics. He moved to Tennessee as a child, where he later became a protégé of Andrew Jackson. Polk's political career began in the Tennessee legislature, and he later served seven terms in the U.S. House of Representatives, becoming Speaker of the House from 1835 to 1839. Afterward, he served as Governor of Tennessee before his election to the presidency in 1844.

Polk's presidency was defined by his firm belief in Manifest Destiny, the idea that American expansion across the continent was inevitable and divinely ordained. He entered office with a clear set of goals: reestablish the Independent Treasury System, reduce tariffs, acquire some or all of Oregon Country, and obtain California and New Mexico from Mexico. Remarkably, he achieved all these objectives within a single term, a testament to his focused and determined leadership.

*Figure 6-10. Output from a ChatGPT-based chatbot*

You shouldn't post this without human review. As you can see, you need to format the content and likely fact-check it, but using a factual URL will help eliminate errors. Once you check for errors, you can then have ChatGPT generate pages at scale while improving quality based on your chosen topic. You can tell ChatGPT to use your formatted original content from the first page generated as a foundation for other content. We don't recommend you take this technique to the extreme of generating SEO programmatic content with generative AI. However, you could significantly speed up the process at scale while still inserting human review and editing into the process.

Going back to the NVIDIA example mentioned earlier, imagine that you have a product being built based on another trending topic or have additional ideas based on trending topics. You can have an agent constantly checking for trending topics in your industry and sending ideas and updates to marketing people. Marketing can then use custom bots and plug-ins to generate pages quickly without waiting for writers to write content. Plug-ins and custom tools can change your content-production time from weeks to hours to keep up with rapidly changing industry trends.

## AI-Assisted Link Attraction and Outreach

SEO is more than generating content on your site. Another area you need to address is marketing and outreach to increase your visibility, attract links, and generate interest in your brand from people reading third-party sites. Focus your efforts on marketing and promotions that develop visibility and recognition from the top sites that cover your market. Avoid traditional SEO link-building strategies that lead to lots of low-quality links—Google just ignores those anyway. Further, spamming the internet with large-scale outreach only causes problems and is a waste of your time and money.

As an example, suppose you have a new product you need to introduce. You can create press releases and reach out to editors on sites that cover your market. The idea is to generate discussion in the market about your product. An agent using generative AI can help.

The agent example in "Building Your Own AI Tools and Plug-ins" on page 186 pulled content from the internet and analyzed it for opportunities. With a different agent, you can have it see what sites link to your competitors. Some of these may be sites that you can attract links from as well as other sites that are like those that link to your competitors. You can also use tools to find backlink gaps yourself. For example, Semrush lets you perform a keyword gap and backlink gap analysis, as shown in Figure 6-11.

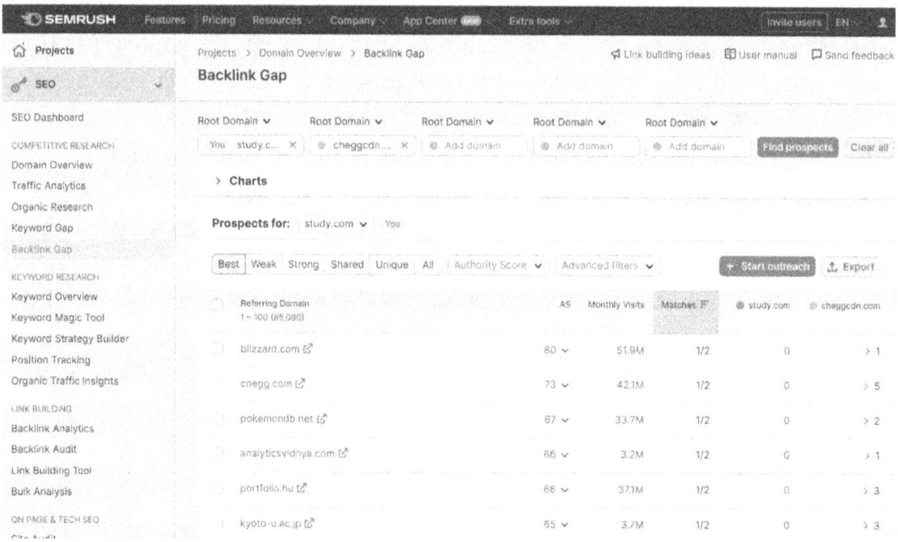

*Figure 6-11. Backlink gap analysis from Semrush*

With a list of backlinks from your competitors, you can then identify your own backlink opportunities. So far, we haven't used generative AI, but we could use it in several different ways. When you want to contact a site to establish a relationship, you can use it to draft email messages. However, don't generate automated email messages and send them without human review. If you create messages that look like AI or have a poor message, you could be blacklisted by that particular publisher.

Third-party backlink analytic tools are best for finding competitor backlinks, but you can feed information from a third-party API (e.g., data from Semrush or Ahrefs) to generative AI. The logic you use depends on the way you program your agent, but you can use an agent to call the API and retrieve data that can be fed to generative AI. For example, the Semrush API can be used to find domain authority for a list of potential backlink locations. With this information, you can then ask generative AI to suggest content or build a list of topic ideas suitable for each site. AI can then identify the editor or person in charge of a target site that an email can be sent to for outreach. Note that you will still want to verify you have the right contacts by human review. This may seem like a minor advantage, but it can save a lot of time when you have significant outreach efforts driving your brand's marketing.

## Creating Video and Audio with AI

Another valuable use of generative AI is image, video, and audio creation. Unfortunately, it can be somewhat obvious when audio and video have been generated by AI. For example, a video of a person speaking might show unnatural mouth movements. AI-generated images tend to be prone to oddities and AI-generated audio can sound robotic, for instance. If you choose to generate this type of content, know that it will need to be heavily edited.

Instead of using generative AI to create video and audio, SEO practitioners can work with AI to improve current audio and video. AI can enhance color grading, program transitions between scenes, and add special effects. When your brand focuses on creating and publishing video rather than text content, this can save hours of editing time for every video.

Other advantages of using AI with video and audio content include writing meta descriptions, transcribing video content, and generating summaries of content for text-based searches. Generative AI is best used for text-based optimizations around video content to satisfy user engagement and quality search signals.

## Using AI to Manage and Optimize Local SEO Listings

Local SEO targets potential customers in a specific geolocation, so it has a different approach than global SEO. Instead of attracting global visitors, your goal is to show up in searches when users want a business or service near them. You could be a single brick-and-mortar store looking for better online visibility or a large-scale brand with hundreds or thousands of locations looking for better reach in each location. Generative AI can help create optimized meta descriptions for your local customers, check your listings to ensure consistent information like addresses and phone numbers, collect customer reviews, and identify competitors ranking for local keywords.

As with global SEO, relying too heavily on automated content without reviewing its output could do more damage than help. With that said, AI can reduce overhead and help with reputation management, tracking local listings, drafting replies to comments and reviews, updating addresses, and alerting business owners of potential dissatisfied customers. The biggest advantage is in AI's predictive analysis, which helps businesses determine the best products to sell during busy seasons and to satisfy ever-changing trends. AI automation changes the game for SEO practitioners responsible for local businesses relying on search visibility in a small region.

A major part of good local SEO is keeping local listings updated with a business's current address, location, and phone number. This information should be consistent across all platforms to send accurate signals to search engines. Search engines must know where the business is located to provide accurate results to users querying for services in their local area. Businesses move, telephone numbers and hours of operation change, and many other factors could also change. You might remember to update an address change on a handful of business listing sites but miss several others. When information is out of sync, that sends low-quality signals to search engines, which affects how high you rank for local search queries.

Using AI automation, local business SEO practitioners can identify sites with outdated information and either send an email to the individual location's manager or owner or draft updates to the content with automated scripts. This automation is the first step, but in the process, AI can scrape a large number of sites, pull ratings and customer comments, and analyze them. The analysis can provide customer sentiment and identify issues. For example, customers might have posted several low ratings complaining about customer service or product quality. AI can identify this issue and send alerts to marketing, SEO practitioners, and PR management to help identify opportunities for improvement.

With enough data extracted from customer activity on a business website, AI can be used to personalize user experiences when they visit. Suppose you have a visitor from a specific city. Data extracted from visitors in this particular city says that most visitors search for a specific item during the summer. As an SEO practitioner, you can instruct developers to display this item more prominently to these users during summer and change the promoted item for the same customer in other seasons.

Voice and image optimization hasn't quite happened yet, but it's something to be aware of for the future. We'll discuss voice and image search in Chapter 8, but keep in mind that using simple voice or image searches will be an expanding area of interest for SEO. Users already can search using images, but that's still primitive. Generative AI can be used to create images on the fly to get your business brand in image searches, offering a new opportunity for visitor traffic. Search using voice has been available for some time, but usage has been relatively low; this will likely also grow.

## AI-Enhanced Reputation Management for SEO

Word of mouth is important for every business, but it's even more important for local businesses. Whether it's a service you offer or a local product, potential customers will likely research reviews before committing to a purchase. Reviews and comments around the web can have a huge impact on revenue. However, a proactive approach to addressing customer issues can turn this around and ensure that the impact is positive.

In "Automating SEO Tasks with AI" on page 176, we talked about agents collecting data online and using it for gap analysis and assisting in content generation using keyword research automation. You can do the same with brand reputation. One of the most powerful uses for AI and machine learning is predictive analysis. In SEO, you can also gain insights into user sentiment.

You can project your brand reputation by monitoring the internet for brand mentions and finding opportunities from user sentiment, positive or negative. The negative reputation from poor reviews can be mitigated by responding to them. You could hire someone full time to respond to negative reviews, especially if the business is a large enterprise, but AI automation can also be your full-time employee and help draft responses to these customer complaints.

Many businesses respond to negative reviews by suggesting that the complainant call customer service. This response is better than nothing, but it's not particularly satisfying, and it's a missed opportunity for the brand. There are opportunities to do so much more with this interaction that helps satisfy not only the complainant but also others watching the conversation online. Brands should view these complaints as an opportunity to show publicly how much they support their customers and project that as part of their brand image.

Instead of having employees scour the internet for brand comments, AI automation can be used to find new brand mentions and draft comments based on users' feedback. Instead of using a canned reply that looks robotic and can actually harm brand reputation, AI can ingest a user's comment and generate a draft customized response for each customer comment.

For example, in Figure 6-12, ChatGPT is given a request to find the latest review for Study.com. This review is positive, but it could be a negative review, too. This prompt can be fed to your RAG system to automatically find reviews at specified intervals (e.g., every day or once a week). You can then take the reviews and formulate a response.

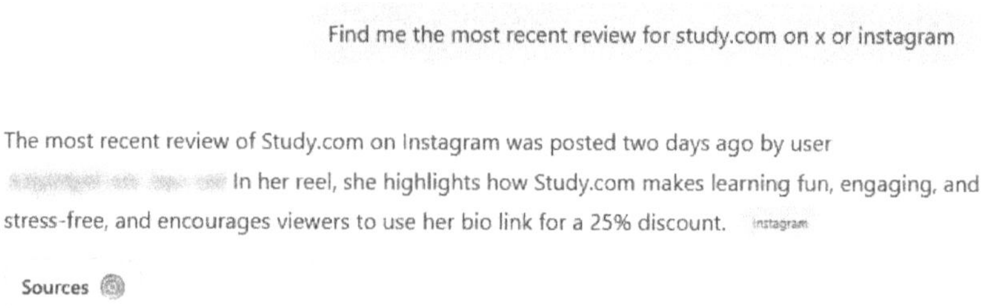

Find me the most recent review for study.com on x or instagram

The most recent review of Study.com on Instagram was posted two days ago by user
███████ ███ ███ In her reel, she highlights how Study.com makes learning fun, engaging, and
stress-free, and encourages viewers to use her bio link for a 25% discount.  Instagram

Sources 🌐

*Figure 6-12. ChatGPT prompt to find the latest review for Study.com*

Figure 6-13 is a generative AI response to the Study.com review. This generated response is appreciative of the positive review, but it could also be a response to a negative review. This example is for a single review, but you can use your RAG agents to track and respond to numerous reviews found around the internet.

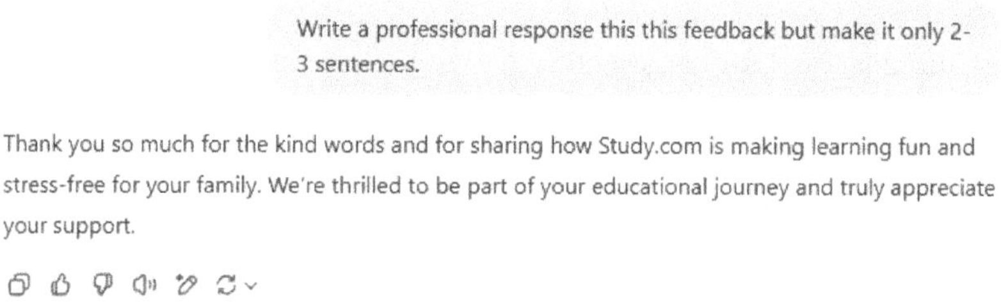

Write a professional response this this feedback but make it only 2-3 sentences.

Thank you so much for the kind words and for sharing how Study.com is making learning fun and
stress-free for your family. We're thrilled to be part of your educational journey and truly appreciate
your support.

🗇 🖒 🖓 🕪 🎤 🗘∨

*Figure 6-13. Generative AI response to an Instagram review for Study.com*

You can also use generative AI for chatbot support. Visitors arriving at your site from search engines can be greeted by a chatbot to help them find a product. While this might not seem like an SEO issue, keeping visitors engaged improves dwell time on a site and reduces the chance of a visitor bouncing to find another site in search. This can affect SEO and directly improve sales, which is the ultimate goal for any SEO or marketing.

Collecting data to gain insights into user sentiment helps with numerous business changes to improve revenue. It can drive new products, suggest changes to products, or let you know when it's time to deprecate a product or service. Marketers and SEO practitioners also can collect data on competitor insights to find out what customers like about a competitor and where the general public wants improvements. Your business can then determine if there are opportunities to create advantages for your own brand based on customer sentiment targeting a competitor.

## Integrating Generative AI with Other Marketing Channels

In the previous section, we talked about using generative AI to analyze customer sentiment on sites where users post reviews or make comments on products. The same can be done with social media. Some review sites even scrape social media accounts for product reviews, so your time could be well spent creating automation scripts to find social media posts that mention your brand and use generative AI to create comments. For example, use generative AI to respond to bad customer experience by suggesting the customer contact customer service. This type of activity is best for reputation management and can span social media and review sites. More broadly, you can use generative AI to discover posts that are relevant to your business and surface them as posts you may want to respond to. Engaging active dialogues on social media and enticing additional visitors to your site can be good for SEO.

PPC is a common traffic generator in marketing. PPC is expensive, but for some brands it's essential to sales. There are a few steps to creating ads: do keyword research to find out what search queries to target, optimize your bids to determine the right price per click, create ad content that drives visitors to your products, schedule ads for optimal times when customers are online, and add tracking to see which ads bring in revenue and which ones don't. As you can imagine, doing all these steps and monitoring ad revenue is a big job. Without optimization, PPC ads can provide a suboptimal return on investment and waste money. Generative AI can help reduce this overhead and make your PPC efforts more cost efficient and optimized for a target audience.

With generative AI, SEO practitioners can create draft ad content based on insights from predictive analytics. The predictive analytics can come from your own agents ingesting data from around the web and from your sales and marketing departments. The predictive analytics results feed optimization of ads and determine when you publish ads and how much you should spend.

Generative AI also handles the draft content creation for human review, so you can reduce the costs of making changes to your ads based on the time of day, the season, results from capturing user activity on landing pages, or general sentiment from scraping reviews from the web. What you do with generative AI depends on your goals, but it can make ad spend and decision making much more precise.

The data you collect from landing pages can be fed to AI and machine learning to make predictions based on user activity. For example, suppose you have a landing page with three product options and the data suggests that more users prefer the blue item out of the three. You can then have generative AI create draft ads (for human review and approval) targeting people with this preference, increasing your ROI.

One more advantage of AI in PPC and marketing is optimization of landing pages. *Heat maps*—common locations where visitors interact—show popular areas where users click on your page. Heat maps are nothing new, but suppose that a heat map shows common areas in a specific menu of your site. You can take this information, feed it to AI and machine learning, and have generative AI suggest changes to your landing page and its content for a more optimized layout. Heat maps already give you ideas for landing-page layouts, but generative AI can make your marketing much more dynamic and quicker to adapt to changes in the way users interact with ads and landing pages.

## Get Started with Generative AI Automation

With so many options for applying generative AI, the first step is to determine what results you want to see. For example, you might wonder if generative AI can help with ad optimization. Your goal might be to increase the brand's conversion rate. Using generative AI, you can suggest updates to landing pages and ads based on data collected from your current pages. You can also use data from sales and user activity to determine your best sellers and any seasonal or trend changes that might affect sales.

With these goals in mind, you can map out your agents and programming design. If you don't have a technical background, you will likely need the help of an engineering team. While a single script might not be too complex, provisioning infrastructure, building multiple agents, and using available APIs can get quite complicated. Engineering teams can help alleviate this overhead and work with your brand to build complete RAG with a system of agents using AI.

As with any generative AI outputs, review of these outputs is critical to ensure that you don't put out incorrect or nonsensical information. You will also need to tweak code or infrastructure to keep up with version changes or trends in your industry.

## Conclusion

In this chapter, we discussed advanced generative AI uses and how to automate many common SEO tasks. With productivity benefits come common pitfalls you must avoid. Automation has its benefits, but it can create serious ranking issues if you don't properly implement and review its output. It's important that you understand the risks associated with the technology so that you can build mitigation strategies into your designs.

As we will discuss in Chapter 7, after systems are in place you must monitor and continually adjust the output based on human reviews. Even when you implement these advanced techniques, you'll still need continual human review. We'll get into the possible risks in the next chapter.

# 7

# AI Risks and Challenges

In Chapter 2, we discussed the limitations of generative AI. This chapter will go over the risks and challenges that derive from those limitations. It's important to understand that limitations and risks are two separate but related concepts. Limitations explain what AI can't do. For example, generative AI can only provide insights using previously published data; it doesn't "know" anything without first ingesting the data that gives it the information it needs.

The limitations of AI are what lead to risks, and these can be devastating to your SEO, brand, and revenue. Various risks can result in revenue-impacting consequences, including litigation, loss of search engine rank, brand damage, and potential penalties. However, many of the risks of AI can be mitigated by careful human reviews. As much as AI reduces overhead and time to perform repeatable SEO tasks, it cannot function well without the critical thinking of human reviewers.

In this chapter, we'll cover some of the common pitfalls you may encounter when using AI and how you can overcome them. If you recall the Gartner Hype Cycle from Chapter 2 (Figure 2-3), one of the phases is disillusionment. Many of AI's pitfalls can contribute to disillusionment, but these challenges can be managed with the right strategies, which we will also discuss in this chapter.

## The Ultimate Risk: Low-Quality Content

The core of an SEO practitioner's job is to produce a site that adds value to the internet by offering users a place to find factual, insightful, engaging content. As soon as you lose sight of that goal, you risk everything, and improper use of AI is a sure way to go down the wrong path. AI is a powerful tool, but with its power comes the responsibility of ensuring that you use it correctly.

Most of this risk results from being able to generate content at scale. If you were producing content at scale years ago, you'd have writers generating several pieces a week. Quality human writers typically produce a relatively low percentage of low-quality content compared to AI, which can generate hundreds—even thousands—of pieces a week. The percentage of low-quality content increases with scale, so the majority of the AI-generated pieces are often vague and unengaging, with what feels like empty text.

Once Google picks up on low-quality signals from your content, you will likely suffer major drops in your search engine traffic. For this reason, we strongly suggest that you don't use generative AI to create content at scale (meaning hundreds of pieces per week) *unless* you have a very large staff to review and fix the myriad problems that you will find within that content.

Google algorithms know when your site may have some low-quality content; it's when your content is unhelpful and unengaging that you start to see a loss in search ranking. Low quality is subjective, but unengaging and unhelpful content often leads to lower user engagement, and this is a significant Google ranking factor. Users leave your page and perform a search to find another site. This behavior sends low-quality signals to algorithms, which leads to a loss of search ranking. Not only are a loss in ranking and Google penalties the biggest risks, but they are also the most difficult to bounce back from. It can take years to recover, and it's possible that you will never regain algorithmic trust. As more content pollutes the internet, algorithmic trust will be much more difficult to obtain, making it harder for smaller brands to compete. Generating massive amounts of content using AI can be initially tempting, but it is highly likely to lead to long-term algorithmic loss in search engine rankings.

As an SEO practitioner, your job is to build pages that answer the intent of a potential customer's search engine query. When generative AI interest boomed in 2023, Google released a statement (*https://oreil.ly/F1VPo*) in February saying that "appropriate use of AI or automation is not against our guidelines." Google never intended that to apply to using generative AI to create poor-quality content.

Let's look at a short example related to SEO. The prompts in Figure 7-1 ask ChatGPT to give the top SEO tip and the top SEO tip for ranking a technology site, and to be specific.

Notice that even though the first request said to be specific, the output is vague. "High quality, user-focused content" is a tip for any site across all industries. The second prompt asks for an SEO tip for ranking a technology site. Notice that the second output is generally the same as the first. Both outputs feel empty and unengaging. If this were a snippet in your content, you would want a human editor to add substance and specificity.

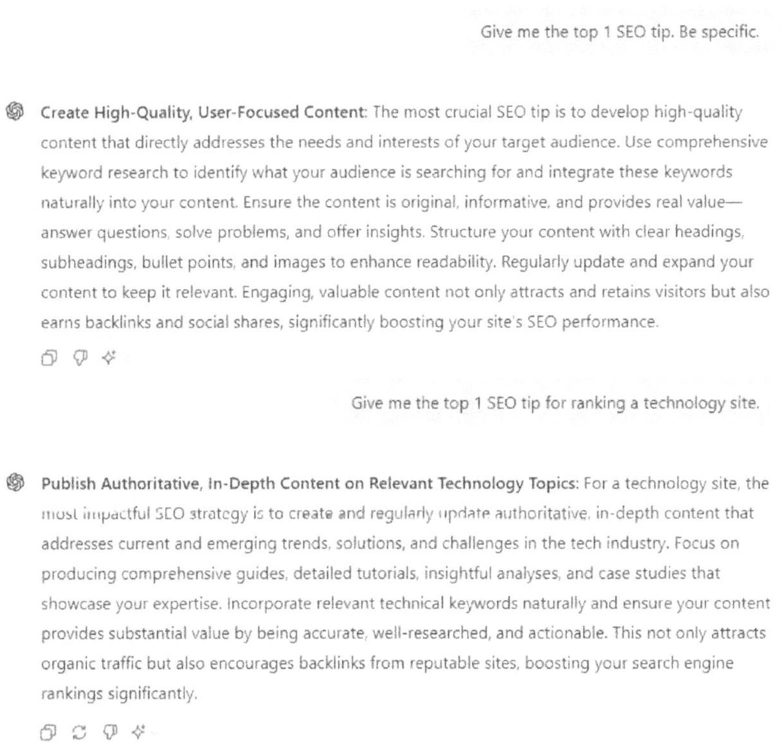

> Give me the top 1 SEO tip. Be specific.

⑯ **Create High-Quality, User-Focused Content:** The most crucial SEO tip is to develop high-quality content that directly addresses the needs and interests of your target audience. Use comprehensive keyword research to identify what your audience is searching for and integrate these keywords naturally into your content. Ensure the content is original, informative, and provides real value—answer questions, solve problems, and offer insights. Structure your content with clear headings, subheadings, bullet points, and images to enhance readability. Regularly update and expand your content to keep it relevant. Engaging, valuable content not only attracts and retains visitors but also earns backlinks and social shares, significantly boosting your site's SEO performance.

⟳ ⟲ ✧

> Give me the top 1 SEO tip for ranking a technology site.

⑯ **Publish Authoritative, In-Depth Content on Relevant Technology Topics:** For a technology site, the most impactful SEO strategy is to create and regularly update authoritative, in-depth content that addresses current and emerging trends, solutions, and challenges in the tech industry. Focus on producing comprehensive guides, detailed tutorials, insightful analyses, and case studies that showcase your expertise. Incorporate relevant technical keywords naturally and ensure your content provides substantial value by being accurate, well-researched, and actionable. This not only attracts organic traffic but also encourages backlinks from reputable sites, boosting your search engine rankings significantly.

⟳ ⟲ ⟲ ✧

*Figure 7-1. ChatGPT output for SEO tips*

Errors by omission are difficult to detect but can be harmful to your brand, especially if your brand relies on being an authority in the industry. Suppose you sell a software as a service (SaaS) product that offers the same two features that your competitor does, but your value-added proposition is an additional feature. This feature was recently introduced, but your competitor has a larger market share. You need to create content that compares your product to your competitor's and use it to introduce your new feature. If you create content using generative AI, it's likely that output will tell users that both SaaS products—yours and your competitor's—have the same two features, but it will omit your newly designed feature. If you automate content creation, you might find that your site's new content is worthless since it doesn't promote the feature that gives your SaaS product a competitive edge. Not only that, but you don't want to just mention this new feature—it should be a significant focus of the content since that's your competitive advantage. While the content is accurate, it's missing critical information for your marketing.

## Note

For a deep dive into examples of errors resulting from AI limitations, see "Limitations of Generative AI" on page 53.

Now let's look at a technical example. Suppose you sell database services and you need to show potential customers that you understand different database engines, specifically MongoDB and Microsoft SQL Server. Let's ask ChatGPT to give us two paragraphs on the differences between the two databases. The output is shown in Figure 7-2.

in two paragraphs, compare the differences between mongo and sql server

MongoDB and SQL Server are both popular database management systems, but they cater to different needs and use cases due to their fundamental differences in data storage and management. SQL Server, developed by Microsoft, is a relational database management system (RDBMS) that uses structured query language (SQL) for defining and manipulating data. It is built on a table-based schema where data is stored in rows and columns, making it ideal for applications requiring complex queries and transactions with strict ACID (Atomicity, Consistency, Isolation, Durability) compliance. SQL Server's structure allows for strong data integrity and the ability to enforce relationships between data entities through foreign keys and constraints, making it suitable for enterprise-level applications with complex data interrelationships.

On the other hand, MongoDB is a NoSQL database that stores data in a flexible, JSON-like format called BSON (Binary JSON). This schema-less design allows for the storage of unstructured or semi-structured data, which can be advantageous for applications requiring rapid iteration and scalability. MongoDB's document-oriented approach means that each document can have a different structure, which provides flexibility and adaptability to changing data requirements. It excels in scenarios involving large volumes of data with diverse formats, such as content management systems, real-time analytics, and big data applications. While it does not inherently enforce relationships between documents, MongoDB offers features like indexing and aggregation that enable efficient querying and data manipulation, albeit with a different paradigm compared to traditional SQL databases.

*Figure 7-2. ChatGPT 4 output comparing MongoDB and SQL Server*

In Figure 7-2, ChatGPT mentions that SQL Server supports a concept called *ACID* (atomicity, consistency, isolation, and durability) and then says that MongoDB offers other advantages. If you look at official MongoDB resource pages, they indicate that MongoDB is also ACID compliant (*https://oreil.ly/diqfG*), as shown in Figure 7-3.

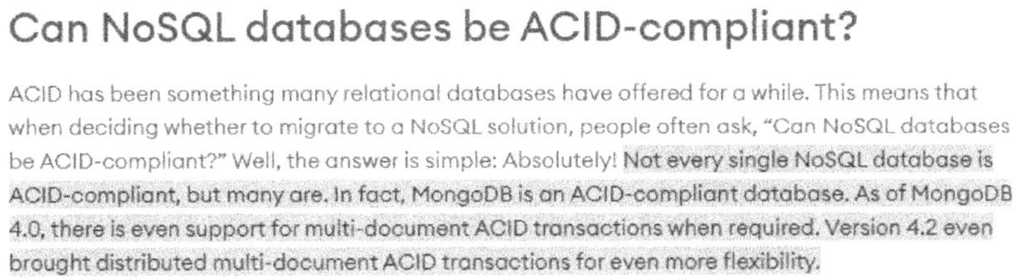

## Can NoSQL databases be ACID-compliant?

ACID has been something many relational databases have offered for a while. This means that when deciding whether to migrate to a NoSQL solution, people often ask, "Can NoSQL databases be ACID-compliant?" Well, the answer is simple: Absolutely! Not every single NoSQL database is ACID-compliant, but many are. In fact, MongoDB is an ACID-compliant database. As of MongoDB 4.0, there is even support for multi-document ACID transactions when required. Version 4.2 even brought distributed multi-document ACID transactions for even more flexibility.

*Figure 7-3. MongoDB resource page information on ACID compliance*

Although the ChatGPT content in Figure 7-2 does not explicitly say that MongoDB is *not* ACID compliant, it omits the fact that MongoDB is ACID compliant, so the information it gives is incorrect. It's easy to see how this type of poor-quality content could cause brand damage by giving potential customers the sense that your brand is not truly an authority in the subject. The ultimate result is fewer sales for your brand and potentially a loss in search engine rankings.

You can use other LLMs to verify information from ChatGPT or cross-reference facts. Figures 7-4 through 7-6 show output for the same query in Claude, Microsoft Copilot, and Gemini.

in two paragraphs, compare the differences between mongo and sql

MongoDB and SQL represent two fundamentally different approaches to data storage and management. SQL (Structured Query Language) databases like MySQL and PostgreSQL use a rigid, predefined schema where data is organized into tables with fixed columns and relationships between them enforced through foreign keys. This structured approach ensures data integrity and consistency, making SQL databases excellent for complex transactions and applications where the data structure is well-defined and unlikely to change frequently. SQL databases also excel at handling complex joins and relationships between data, making them particularly suitable for applications like financial systems or inventory management where data consistency is crucial.

MongoDB, on the other hand, is a NoSQL database that stores data in flexible, JSON-like documents. This schema-less approach means fields can vary between documents and data structure can be modified easily over time without requiring migrations. MongoDB's flexible structure makes it particularly well-suited for applications with rapidly changing data requirements, large amounts of unstructured data, or where horizontal scaling is needed. However, this flexibility comes at the cost of not having built-in support for complex joins between collections, and transactions are not as robust as in SQL databases. MongoDB is often chosen for content management systems, real-time analytics, and applications where the data structure might evolve significantly over time.

 Copy ⟳ Retry ⌂ ⤺

Claude can make mistakes. Please double-check responses.

*Figure 7-4. Claude output comparing MongoDB and SQL Server*

in two paragraphs, compare the differences between mongo and sql

MongoDB and SQL databases fundamentally differ in their approach to data storage and retrieval. SQL databases, such as MySQL, PostgreSQL, and Oracle, are relational databases that store data in tables with rows and columns. These databases follow a structured schema, which means the data structure must be defined beforehand. SQL databases are known for their ACID (Atomicity, Consistency, Isolation, Durability) properties, ensuring data integrity and reliability, making them suitable for complex transactional applications. Additionally, SQL databases use structured query language (SQL) for querying and managing the data, providing powerful capabilities for data manipulation and retrieval.

On the other hand, MongoDB is a NoSQL database that stores data in flexible, JSON-like documents. Unlike SQL databases, MongoDB does not require a predefined schema, allowing for more dynamic and scalable data structures. This flexibility makes MongoDB ideal for applications that handle large volumes of unstructured or semi-structured data, such as real-time analytics, content management systems, and IoT applications. MongoDB also provides horizontal scaling capabilities, making it easier to distribute data across multiple servers. While MongoDB may not offer the same level of ACID compliance as SQL databases, it provides a different set of benefits for modern, agile development environments where schema flexibility and scalability are crucial.

Let me know if you have any questions about this!

*Figure 7-5. Microsoft Copilot output comparing MongoDB and SQL Server*

in two paragraphs, compare the differences between mongo
and sql

MongoDB and SQL databases represent two fundamentally different approaches to data
management. SQL databases, like MySQL or PostgreSQL, are relational databases that organize
data into tables with predefined schemas. This structure enforces data consistency and integrity
through relationships between tables, making them ideal for applications with complex data
relationships and strict data accuracy requirements, such as financial systems or inventory
management. They use SQL (Structured Query Language) for defining and manipulating data,
which is a powerful and standardized language for querying and managing structured data.

In contrast, MongoDB is a NoSQL database that uses a document-oriented data model. It stores
data in flexible, JSON-like documents within collections, allowing for dynamic schemas and easier
handling of unstructured or semi-structured data. This flexibility makes MongoDB well-suited for
applications with evolving data structures, such as content management systems, social media
platforms, or real-time analytics. MongoDB's query language is based on JavaScript, offering a
more intuitive and developer-friendly approach for those familiar with web development.
Additionally, MongoDB's architecture allows for horizontal scaling, making it easier to handle large
volumes of data and high traffic loads.

👍 👎 ⟳ ⦉ ⋮

*Figure 7-6. Gemini output comparing MongoDB and SQL Server*

To overcome errors of omission, you need a true SME who can identify
the missing pieces, understand where to look for them, and validate that the
information is correct. In this example, a reviewer who understands databases
is required to know that both databases are ACID compliant and to validate the
information on the vendor's site.

When creating content at scale, remember that your primary goal is to offer
value to the user. The meat of the issue is low-quality content, and the other risks
we cover in the rest of this chapter feed into those concerns about low-quality
content.

## Speed of Publishing: Faster Is Not Always Better for SEO

Hiring writers was always a big overhead cost and a time-consuming endeavor
for SEO practitioners, so the thought of having AI become one hundred writers
overnight is tempting. As Google (and other search engines) continue to evolve
and attempt to control the mass publication of AI-generated content, it's important to realize that faster publication doesn't always mean improved quality and
better search engine placement. As a matter of fact, if you previously published

one or two articles a week and are now suddenly publishing hundreds of articles a week, you might be sending the wrong quality signals to search algorithms.

As we discussed in previous sections, Google downranks low-quality AI-generated content. AI models used to generate content aren't at the point where no human editor is necessary, but large numbers of organizations tried to use it that way anyway in 2024, and as a result, we saw massive chaos in search engines indexing misinformation on the internet because all of the low-quality content that was published. Users complained, and Google rolled back its initial stance on AI-generated content being fine for users and ranking.

A component of search algorithms is the concept of *trust*. Trust is often measured in the age of a site and the long-term quality signals sent to the search engine. For example, if your site is BMW and you're trying to rank for car-related content, Google will likely trust your site much more than newer sites. We've observed that Google has rolled back changes and returned to trusting older long-term brand sites in spaces where there is a lot of AI-generated noise from massive content publishing. Google trust factors are difficult to measure, but you can avoid downranking by always reviewing your AI-generated content.

Every site has its low-quality content, but that should be kept to a minimum. If you publish hundreds of new articles a week after you traditionally published only a few articles a week, that will likely send low-quality signals to search engines. The idea of trust is to consistently but slowly ramp up production to ensure that quality content remains a primary goal. Scaling up slowly will avoid sending any red flags to quality algorithms. As an example, you might have a 50:1 ratio of quality content, where 1 out of 50 articles sends low-quality signals. If you ramp up automated content too much without checking for quality, your quality ratio might rapidly change to 60:30, meaning nearly half your content is low quality. A worse ratio will probably affect the overall search ranking of your site.

## Copyright: Unique Content Doesn't Mean You Own It

Your content may pass plagiarism checkers, but AI puts a new spin on copyright. Because AI generates content based on the writing of others, you're creating content that isn't truly your own, even though that sequence of words is not found anywhere else on the internet. Content written in the same tone, voice, and style as another author could be considered copyright infringement. We say "could" be copyright infringement because as of the writing of this book, lawsuits are still pending.

Eight large, well-known publishers are suing OpenAI—the creators of ChatGPT—for copyright infringement (*https://oreil.ly/TQlnf*). At the foundation of the lawsuits is the claim that ChatGPT content uses their original work and their journalists' original ideas to generate similar content. The lawsuit claims that OpenAI used their work to train models, which begs the question if AI can ever generate original content if some data it ingests is unusable.

Copyright infringement is still an unknown factor in future regulations, but SEO practitioners should ensure that they neither prompt AI to create content in the same style and tone as any other author nor create content using a single source of information. Neglecting this could increase the likelihood of infringement lawsuits (*https://oreil.ly/Jf9mb*). Some lawsuits such as *Concord Music Group, Inc. v. Anthropic PBC* and *The New York Times v. Microsoft and OpenAI* provide the courts with output that copies original works verbatim. LLM providers are contesting the allegations (*https://oreil.ly/QiEBt*) and claim that "regurgitation" of content is a bug rather than a feature. SEO practitioners using generative AI to produce content can't copyright it either (*https://oreil.ly/X_eqE*), which can cause issues if your own content is stolen.

To avoid copyright infringement, diversify your sources and provide references—with a link or footnote—to sources used in your content. Some SEO professionals choose to work with multiple LLMs to diversify output and validate information. For example, you might use ChatGPT to generate content and use Claude to verify that content. You can also specify using multiple sources in your prompts and ask ChatGPT to provide a list of sources for its content.

## Plagiarism: Did You Write This Content?

Every teacher has students who try to pass off plagiarized content as their own. Generative AI can be your bad student if you use it to create content without thoroughly checking it. Instead of having one writer produce plagiarized content, AI could be the equivalent of one hundred writers producing plagiarized content. For SEO practitioners, having the same content as multiple other sites lowers quality signals sent to search engines and could affect your search ranking.

Plagiarism on the internet is a bit different than academic plagiarism. Academically, you can't rewrite a whitepaper from another researcher and call it your own just because it passes plagiarism checkers. This activity is still plagiarism. But the internet works differently than academics. The same idea is often written about dozens of times on the internet. Your content strategies might overlap these same ideas, but you want to add value that can't be found in other brands' content strategies. "Value" is subjective and depends on your target audience, but your goal should be to provide information related to the search query and a call to action to instruct the reader where to go next. This will offer value to readers and search engines, which will in turn improve your ranking and trust signals.

When you have writers working for you, you check their content for plagiarism. An example of a tool that does this is Copyscape (*https://www.copy scape.com*), but you can find many other tools using your favorite search engine. These tools aren't perfect, but they provide a good first check to ensure that your writers aren't plagiarizing. You should also compare your content with what's already published on the internet. You can copy and paste full or partial sentences into Google to see if large blocks of content were plagiarized by the writer.

Separately, you should check that your writers are not using generative AI tools to create content and then calling it their own work. As we discussed in Chapter 3, you run the risk that writers won't do a great job of reviewing the content for errors, omissions, copyright infringement, and the like. There are many tools out there for checking if the content has been written by AI, such as Copyleaks and ZeroGPT. See "AI-Detection Tools" on page 96 for a longer list.

### Warning

We should note that tools that check content to see if it was written by AI can be notoriously inaccurate. As a matter of fact, AI-generation checkers say that the US Constitution was written by AI (*https://oreil.ly/6sYiP*). Nevertheless, you should perform these checks as they may flag some issues. Be aware that they will also sometimes flag content that was not written by AI and say that it was. So treat the output of these tools as directionally correct, but have humans verify their assessments.

Have editors on your staff review the work of your writers to look for other issues indicating that writers may be taking excessive shortcuts using generative AI to create content. If you have the development capacity, the best way to guarantee that content is original is to use a CMS (or equivalent technology) that requires writers to write in the tool, without copying and pasting from external documents. You can then employ keystroke biometrics algorithms or tools like TypingDNA (*https://oreil.ly/ugIvQ*) or Typing AI (*http://typing.ai*) that fingerprint the writer's speed and keystroke dynamics to make sure they are doing original work.

AI-generated content takes input from other sources, but it can be used to create unique content when summarizing something that a person has written. Citing sources will give proper credit to the original author. LLMs now include links to original sources so that you can give attribution when posting content to your site.

Originality checkers still can't identify AI-generated content with 100% accuracy, but using them will help flag potential plagiarism and AI-generated content to verify that your writers aren't using AI. For all AI-generated content, you should have a human editor check it for errors, omissions, and awkward wording.

## Automation Complacency: You Can't "Set It and Forget It"

AI is a powerful automation tool. We discussed some automation use cases in Chapter 6. You can perform so much with AI—either with external tools that work with AI (e.g., Google Analytics) or by building your own tools. For example, you might use AI in Microsoft Excel macros to gather data and create descriptions or identify trends. You can do a lot with AI that gives you a competitive edge, such as day-to-day automated information about competitor rankings or a gap analysis between a competitor's ranking and their published content versus your own published content.

Automating in SEO with AI is essential for efficiency, but AI changes rapidly (primarily due to the extremely high pace of innovation in AI and its popularity). As more bugs and innovations are introduced, AI companies will adapt and offer new models that provide significantly better results. Chapter 2 covers the evolution of popular models, and there will likely be another iteration soon after the release of this book.

Changes to AI should benefit users, including SEO executives, but you should ensure that your automation scripts take these changes into account. AI automation should be consistently reviewed for any industry changes that could affect accuracy in output. For example, Google struck a $60 million deal (*https://oreil.ly/Yltlo*) with Reddit to use Reddit content to help train its generative AI tools. Reddit has millions of users, and Gemini can benefit from the human-generated content. If you have any kind of automation based on content generation by Gemini, the changes to Reddit and its content "tone" can dramatically influence the type of content created from it. This tone and messaging could diverge from your internal policies, product voice, or audience concerns.

Another common automation opportunity is using AI for competitor analysis or backlink opportunities. Both can take hours out of a single SEO practitioner's time, so using AI greatly reduces overhead without eliminating essential research. Using automation, you can scan competitors' links, review their latest content strategies, get a list of their backlinks, and apply this research to building your own strategies. It might even give you insight into your competitors' seasonal habits and product launches. AI models and products continually change, and in doing so they affect your reports. Your SEO team will still need to review this work for accuracy, but it can significantly speed up the process of doing the work.

However, if you do not update your own scripts and monitor the results, you could be skewing results unknowingly. In a scenario where you use generative AI for competitor analysis, perhaps it picks up new domains that weren't being analyzed before, or changes to a site aren't being used in current models. This scenario again represents the need to always work with human reviewers for generative AI output. Human reviewers can check for inaccuracies and awkward word choices, and they can edit content to have a more conversational tone. Small changes from human reviewers can make content much more engaging to readers and avoid inaccuracies. The same is true for any automation tools used in critical research and reporting.

If you fall into the trap of "set it and forget it," you will eventually generate low-quality content at scale, or you will mistakenly target queries that could be too costly for their ROI. Let's say that you create content based on the top three ranking competitors. Your AI automation may scan competitor pages, extract keywords, and create content based on a gap analysis. But it likely won't fully understand the context of what pages it makes sense to create.

For example, what if Google's AIOs take a majority of screen real estate on mobile, so users are forced to scroll a long way to see the search listing for your site? Users may not want to look that far. In addition, the AIO may answer the question well enough that users don't bother to scroll down the page.

If you generate a large number of articles based on a single gap analysis, you might be deploying content for a query that will never result in a positive ROI. For example, if you use Google Analytics to track traffic and engagement, you might notice much fewer clicks on your call to action or fewer organic search visitors. It can be costly if you have infrastructure and other expensive events (e.g., API queries from third-party vendors) without a return on your investment. This is one example of why you should always review automation and never inherently trust it even if the AI results are correct for most of your automated events.

## The SEO Nightmare: Losing Search Engine Rank or Google Penalties

Losing rankings (or receiving a manual penalty) is the bane of an SEO practitioner's existence. These downfalls occur quickly, and fixing the issue can require months of work. Some sites never fully recover. To avoid this nightmare, SEO practitioners strive to follow Google's guidelines while still breaking barriers with unique and innovative strategies to help their brand.

Losing rankings and Google penalties are two separate phenomena. *Losing rankings* means you have negative factors affecting algorithmic trust and quality signals. A *penalty* is manual action on your site meant to keep your site from ranking well. Both are difficult to fix, but they require two separate strategies. Losing rankings requires reviewing your site for low-quality signals and technical issues, but a penalty means that a serious violation of Google's policies must be remedied.

Google wants to integrate generative AI into the search results, but it also knows that human users must be satisfied with the search results. A poor user experience would push users to Google's competitors like Bing and other LLMs with a direct answer, and this would destroy brand reputation for Google's dominant search engine. Contrasting with this is the existence of market pressures caused by the massive buzz around generative AI. If Google isn't seen as a leader in this area, this could directly affect its overall reputation as the technology leader in search. It's a confusing conflict of interest for SEO practitioners who might assume that anything AI is looked on favorably by Google engineers.

Then there is the matter of how Google views AI-generated content. In February 2023, Google released guidance on AI-generated content (*https://oreil.ly/F1VP0*) indicating that its main concern with content was its quality, not whether it was written by AI. However, Google knows content created by generative AI doesn't offer any unique value beyond what is already contained on the web and is often of poor quality unless it's heavily edited by a human SME. Yet many sites will go ahead and publish content written by generative AI without such review. For that reason, Google may try to detect AI-generated content, and it's likely that Google has AI-detection tools that are more advanced than the tools that are currently commercially available in the market.

For example, in March 2024 Google announced a new update to its core search functionality (*https://oreil.ly/PvyjN*), promising that less "spammy" content would be released. Rollouts happened in May 2024, and many SEO practitioners who did not heed the warning saw a penalty in their Search Console. The penalty mentioned "spammy" content, and SEO practitioners with poor-quality, AI-generated content experienced a massive drop in search visibility.

Despite the risks, most of Google's announcements at its Google I/O conference in 2024 (*https://oreil.ly/hrds3*) focused on AI because that is the hot new technology area. Google had AI for video, text, art, scripting, storytelling, health, and science. Everything in Google I/O had an element of AI to it, but the search engine engineers emphasized the importance of user engagement. Suffice to say that Google supports generative AI, but site owners must maintain quality content, even if it's generated by AI. Google's search engine users are most important to Google's growth and sustainability. Therefore, SEO practitioners should have human reviewers for all content uploaded to their sites.

## Compliance and Changes in Regulations

The introduction of ChatGPT in 2023 brought AI to the forefront as the next "must-have" technology. AI has received a lot of attention from media outlets, SEO practitioners, marketing people, and businesses looking to leverage it for their own benefit. Governments took notice and are coming up with ways to mitigate risks and oversee ethics and legal compliance related to data usage and AI-generated content.

At the time of writing, the EU had passed the AI Act (*https://oreil.ly/c4ST6*) to oversee the creation of AI products and the ethics behind services. The AI Act focuses on accountability and transparency for technology involved in AI. The US will likely follow suit with state-level regulations (*https://oreil.ly/-mL_h*). For example, Vermont created a Division of Artificial Intelligence (*https://oreil.ly/SGqan*) to identify the ways AI affects Vermont residents. Future regulations in other states are highly probable.

Because AI integration is relatively new, regulations are still in their infancy and will likely develop rapidly. What regulations look like will change as AI evolves. It's important to keep notified of the latest regulations surrounding AI and your industry. Some regulations will be specific to your organization or clients. For example, there is likely to be more regulation overseeing health care as AI is introduced to health care Internet of Things, patient diagnosis, and tools used for treatments. This is just one example, but any industry looking to integrate AI will likely run into compliance issues and regulations to oversee the way AI can be marketed and used. To ensure compliance, you can hire consultants to audit your environment and text for any privacy or regulation concerns. If your business supports multiple countries, you might need auditors with knowledge of EU or other country regulations.

## Removing Bias: Human Emotions Are Not Objective

For AI to be effective, you need it to be neutral, bipartisan, and unbiased. *Bias* is a phenomenon in AI where output takes stereotypes or human subjectivity into account. It usually focuses on human biases, but bias can take different forms. For example, if you want to determine if someone should be accepted for a home loan, AI should not take race or religion into consideration even if this information is a part of the dataset. An SEO practitioner generating content for a site needs to ensure that output does not have bias. Bias is difficult to avoid because it's human nature to inject our own experiences and opinions into content. A second human review can help avoid publishing content with bias.

Most people watch for human bias and demographic stereotypes. Bias in AI can be a compliance issue, so it can result in monetary fines for certain businesses if it isn't caught before decision making. As an example, US financial loan regulations specify the types of data that cannot be included in prediction analysis for mortgage approvals. Should an SEO practitioner unknowingly use this type of data to market or falsely advertise, that could lead to potential legal troubles.

Let's look at the results from a query in ChatGPT. The query asks, "What is the best security tool?" This question is likely too open for generative AI, but you might be creating a draft article for a cybersecurity company to compare some tools and drive search engine traffic to your site. OpenAI, the vendor for ChatGPT, is partnered with Microsoft. Microsoft has invested more than $13 billion (*https://oreil.ly/CxLlb*) in OpenAI since its partnership in 2019. It should be no surprise, then, when ChatGPT has biased output favoring Microsoft-based tools, as can be seen in Figure 7-7.

what is the best security tool?

 The best security tool can vary depending on your specific needs and environment, but one highly recommended option for comprehensive protection is **Microsoft Defender for Endpoint**. This tool provides advanced threat protection and endpoint detection and response capabilities. It integrates well with other Microsoft services, offering real-time threat analysis, automated investigation and remediation, and robust reporting features.

Key Features:

1. **Advanced Threat Protection**: Identifies and stops attacks with built-in AI and machine learning.

2. **Endpoint Detection and Response (EDR)**: Offers detailed insights into threats and their potential impact.

3. **Automated Remediation**: Automatically resolves detected issues, reducing the burden on IT teams.

4. **Integration with Microsoft Services**: Seamlessly works with Windows, Azure, and other Microsoft products for enhanced security across your ecosystem.

*Figure 7-7. ChatGPT 4.0 output for the query "What is the best security tool?"*

Bias is difficult to identify, especially when it's an unknown bias injected into data used for generative AI. You should run tests on your own output and have human reviewers validate your results. Data should be diverse, but this step also assumes that you are building your own tools. For smaller businesses, having a development team isn't always feasible, but you should manually audit generative AI output to identify any potential bias flaws. For most businesses, building your own LLM is out of budget, but you can build a knowledge base from preexisting LLMs. It also helps to use trusted data sources. For example, the CIA offers *The World Factbook* (*https://oreil.ly/9LdDT*) to help data scientists and businesses collect accurate, unbiased data on some topics.

In most SEO environments, you don't control the data, but you can control the output. It's best to have a second person review your results or compare them against results from other tools. Not only can multiple result sets help you identify bias, but they can also help optimize your reporting. For example, you might discover better backlinking opportunities from one tool's results as compared with another tool's. As we have mentioned several times before, AI cannot replace human critical thinking, so your output should always be monitored and reviewed to ensure that you have the best results for your sites.

## Theft of Intellectual Property

A challenge in the digital landscape is the difficulty controlling who can access your intellectual property, particularly sophisticated AI bots designed to scrape the internet and steal content. While preventing such activity is often impossible, SEO practitioners should be aware of this threat, especially when it comes to protecting their brand's reputation.

Content theft can negatively affect your SEO efforts in several ways. For example, a malicious actor might republish your content on their own site in the hopes of ranking for your target keywords. A copycat site could use your brand's reputation to fraudulently sell products and services, stealing your revenue. One way to combat this is to use AI to help you monitor the web to detect content theft.

Generative AI introduces new dimensions to content theft. Malicious actors can now leverage tools to not just copy but also re-create and repurpose your content in ways that may be harder to detect and combat. In the US, you can always try reporting the problem to the National Intellectual Property Rights Coordination Center, but this is a manual process, and having to report each incident can become an overwhelming task.

Then there is the flip side of the coin—if you are using AI to generate logos, characters, and images, make sure that the content created does not accidentally infringe on a trademark.

## Impact of AI Limitations on SEO

Google has always pushed quality over quantity, but generative AI has made quantity much more attainable. A study by WebFX on generative AI and its impact on search ranking (*https://oreil.ly/yVsdZ*) highlights the advantages and disadvantages of content generation.

Advantages:

- Content creation is more efficient and faster, even with a human editor involved.
- Content creation is more cost-effective without the time and human resources needed to generate new ideas and content.
- You can generate content ideas continuously rather than relying on human research.
- You can pool research and fact-checking into a single location.

Disadvantages:

- There is no personal touch. In human-written content, personal experiences and anecdotes often help engage readers. AI-generated content has none of these traits and can sound robotic.

- It's important to fact-check and review all AI-generated content to avoid errors. Error by omission is also a common disadvantage, meaning content might be technically accurate in what it says but a lack of context or additional information makes the statement misinformation.

- Generative AI models are trained on current data, so the content created is on evergreen knowledge. You won't get any current news or new information that the model has not been trained on. Models are trained only a few times a year, so information might be outdated.

The WebFX case study indicates that AI-generated content could harm ranking, especially if your pages are already ranking. The example given was a lawn care site already ranking for targeted keywords. AI-generated content was added to the site, but it was regurgitated information already on the web. Pages with AI-generated content not only saw minimal traffic but eventually lost 100% of their ranking after a short time.

It's important to remember that Google hires contractors to review ranking pages. Google asks contractors to evaluate the EEAT of content (*https://oreil.ly/ Lo1fr*), which means that content must display experience, expertise, authoritativeness, and trustworthiness. The same WebFX study said that a financial site with mostly AI-generated content saw a 99.3% drop in ranking after the November 2023 EEAT core update. AI-generated content doesn't usually exhibit strong EEAT, so have your human editors determine if content could be considered high quality based on EEAT.

## Conclusion

In this chapter, we went over how you can overcome some of the common pitfalls when using AI. Succumbing to these risks can have devastating effects on your brand and revenue. Here's a brief recap:

*Low-quality content*
Whether it's generating images, video or text, AI has its limitations, and a human reviewer should be injected into your procedures to ensure content quality. The main risk of poor generative AI strategies is low-quality

content. It might not seem like the worst risk, but the consequences can be significant (e.g., loss of search rank or search engine penalties, which both result in fewer sales).

*Copyright and plagiarism*

Generative AI platforms ingest data from the internet, so output can be too similar to the original content. Several ethical and legal issues stem from this challenge.

*Automation complacency*

Automation is one of AI's greatest benefits, but it's not a "set it and forget it" application. We discussed SEO automation in Chapter 6. AI results must be constantly reviewed by humans, regardless of whether you use it for just a few pieces of content or you deploy it at scale.

*Google authority loss and penalties*

User experience is key to following Google's search engine guidelines and ranking well, but analysis shows that AI-produced content published without detailed human review results in poor user experiences and can cause your search rankings to plummet.

*Compliance*

Is the content output compliant with local and federal laws? The EU passed the AI Act, which aims to regulate AI and its products. The AI Act focuses on two concerns: it bans social scoring similar to China's social scoring system, and it regulates CV (resume) ranking tools, which must follow strict regulations. US regulations are soon to follow.

*Biases*

For large agencies or businesses with the staff to create their own models and tools, it's critical that output is tested for any biases that can creep into your content and cause issues with readers and local laws. For example, feed ChatGPT the query "Should marijuana be fully legalized nationwide in the US?" and notice that the response doesn't give you a direct answer.

*Theft of intellectual property*

An uncontrollable but related issue is the use of AI to bypass common blocks (e.g., *robots.txt*) on traffic or bots used to steal your intellectual property. For example, if you use *robots.txt* to block traffic, you have no guarantee that crawlers will honor it. After stealing your content, AI can be used to create intellectual property like your own without detection.

This chapter is meant to inform rather than deter. You need to know what to avoid and integrate these challenges into your SEO strategies. These challenges also shape the future of AI, how it will evolve, and the regulations surrounding it. The next chapter will cover the future of AI and SEO and what you can look forward to (or possibly avoid) as you continue using it.

# 8

# The Future of Generative AI and SEO

Generative AI is still evolving, so our approach to using it with search engines and SEO must change as well. By identifying emerging trends and potential enhancements, you can better prepare for the future and stay ahead of your competitors.

In this chapter, we'll examine emerging trends in generative AI and their implications for the future of SEO. We'll explore how these trends will reshape our day-to-day SEO practices. Our primary objective will be to equip SEO professionals with the foresight necessary to anticipate and adapt to these changes.

A common question among SEO professionals is "Will generative AI search steal massive market share from Google?" This chapter will address those concerns and provide an expert view on the future of generative AI and search engines.

## Anticipating the Evolving Landscape of Generative AI and SEO

Until now, we've discussed the many advantages and limitations of AI as it currently functions. LLMs and generative AI will continue to evolve, and you must account for those changes in your future SEO strategies. In this section, we'll discuss what you can expect of generative AI in the future and how that will affect SEO professionals and business owners.

The first area where we foresee changes is in the overall quality of AI-generated content. Text content will sound more humanlike. As a result, marketing content—including ad copy—will be more appealing to customers. Images and videos will look more realistic and natural. SEO practitioners will find it easier to develop content. This doesn't change the fact that AI-generated content will still need human oversight. As we've emphasized throughout this book, if you do not have a human reviewer, you risk your brand's reputation by putting out content rife with misinformation and inaccuracies or content that sounds too robotic to resonate with users. In addition, you have lost the opportunity to put forth your organization's perspective and insights.

Second, we'll see new regulations and laws regarding the use of generative AI. Laws currently are not set up to protect non-human-generated art and text. In the future, we'll see more regulations to control what can be owned and what constitutes copyright infringement as artists' work is used to train AI models. More laws will oversee and limit the use of other art to generate images. However, SEO practitioners will continue to use generative AI to create basic logos and for image search and editing. For more details, see "Copyright Concerns" on page 53.

Third, Google will remain a search engine and generative AI leader, for reasons we'll discuss in the following sections of this chapter. Users will see more AI-generated content alongside traditional search results, which could affect trust and search engine ranking. Companies that offer users informational content will need to focus on getting their content to become one of the sources for AI-generated responses in addition to ranking in traditional search results. Companies will compete for their pages to be used as part of the AI search overviews.

Fourth, SEO practitioners and developers should better utilize generative AI to increase the velocity of coding websites and desktop and mobile applications. From user interface designs developed for better optimization and engagement to backend code snippets, generative AI can help get your websites and applications in front of customers sooner.

Finally, generative AI will streamline the work of SEO practitioners and video producers. AI models will get better at processing videos and producing accurate subtitles, alternative text, and transcripts. It's also foreseeable that translations of video into other languages will improve.

Although switching to a focus on generative AI results may sound overwhelming, remember that your primary focus should continue to be on quality and providing value to users. Having authoritative content will become more important than in previous years because generative AI tool vendors will strive to use trustworthy content. SEO professionals will need SMEs and careful oversight of any generative AI content to ensure that it meets Google's authoritative content expectations.

## Will Generative AI Search Overtake or Replace Search Engines?

The fundamental goal of SEO—to enhance a website's visibility and ranking in search engines in order to gain relevant traffic to the website—faces a significant shift with the rise of generative AI. However, it's unlikely that generative AI will completely replace search engines.

Google will probably lose some market share to ChatGPT and other LLMs, but not a significant amount. Generative AI requires massive amounts of data, and Google has the most data in the world from its years of cataloging the web, understanding user intent and relevancy, and identifying authorities on a wide range of topics. In addition, Google has built a massive repository of facts called the Knowledge Graph (*https://oreil.ly/IwSxk*), which provides it with a way to validate content accuracy.

Many users will move to using generative AI instead of search engines to find information. For example, when a user uses a search engine to look for pizza places, their query might ask Google to find pizza restaurants close to their location. This query doesn't always return an exact match. The top three ranking restaurants might have long wait times or not have the user's preferred menu item. These specifics are likely found in the customer feedback, and generative AI ingests and processes feedback. Users will then go to their favorite AI tool (e.g., ChatGPT or Copilot) to ask questions rather than rely on search engine results.

In contrast, a user can ask generative AI to return three pizza restaurants. Suppose the LLM returns the same three results as Google. The user can then ask the LLM to give them results based on other ingested information like wait times, menu items, and customer feedback that wouldn't be part of on-site content. This gives SEO professionals another type of information to target on their sites: information that addresses follow-up questions. Authoritative content that focuses on these kinds of follow-up questions could help sites become a reference in an LLM output.

When it comes to search on smartphones, Google has already integrated AI (Gemini) into Android. Most Android smartphones work with Google AI when users initiate search assistance. Instead of targeting web page content, SEO practitioners will need to focus on injecting their brands into recommendations offered by smartphone AI assistants. These assistants may be even smarter in the future and will begin giving suggestions before the user asks. For example, suppose a smartphone user regularly buys flowers on a specific day for their spouse's birthday. The assistant could recommend flower stores before the user performs a search. SEO practitioners will need to create strategies for being one of the top—or *the* top—recommendations.

In this section, we'll examine how AI will continue to affect SEO. We'll look at how AI overviews will impact search traffic, the need to optimize for generative engines, the influence of query intent on results, and how AI will affect certain business models.

## THE IMPACT OF AI OVERVIEWS ON SEARCH TRAFFIC

Being in the top three search results does not give you the same click-through traffic as before AI integration, but being a source in generative AI answers can increase search traffic. For most informational queries you type into Google, you'll notice that the AI-generated answer takes up much of the real estate at the top of the results page.

Figure 8-1 shows what a desktop user sees after typing a query into Google Search. As you can see, AI-generated answers take up most of the screen, and only one link is shown. Results two and three—previously considered a good ranking—are not above the fold. The AI-generated answer is likely enough to satisfy many users, so the potential for informational queries to send traffic to websites via traditional web results is much lower.

### Note

"Above the fold" refers to search links showing up on the screen without requiring users to scroll down. Links shown below the fold have a tremendous drop in CTR. SEO professionals aim to keep their web links above the fold for better organic traffic.

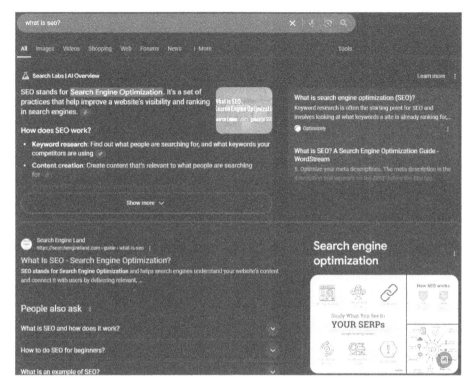

*Figure 8-1. Current Google layout for search results in Windows and Chrome*

An article in *Search Engine Land* (*https://oreil.ly/xYa4S*) notes that AI-generated answers from search queries lowered organic traffic by 18%–64% and reduced CTR by 60%. Predictive algorithms are not new, but predictive algorithms used for generative AI could be Google's next move for its search strategy. For example, some number-one results have been pushed down by 640 pixels, but this ranges between 200 and 2,000 pixels depending on Google's experiments, according to the same *Search Engine Land* article. When your site is affected, you may see the same position ranking for your keywords and impressions, but the CTR will be much lower, and therefore traffic to your site will be significantly affected.

Because of these layout changes, being in the top three search results—or even on the first page—is no longer good enough. You need to be a part of the AIOs: the AI-generated answers for informational queries at the top of Google SERPs. (We discussed AIOs in more detail in Chapter 2.) As you can see in Figure 8-1, the right side of the AIO section contains reference links. The future of SEO will be to include your brand in these reference links. This strategy is referred to as *generative engine optimization (GEO)*, which we will discuss in more detail shortly.

SEO practitioners will battle for placement in Google's AIOs at the top of a user's search results. Google launched AIOs at scale in November–December 2024, and the search giant is testing results from the experiment. Because of the scale of the launch, Google should be able to systematically improve the quality of AIOs.

However, if Google doesn't send material traffic to the websites from which it sources its content, publishers will lose the incentive to provide access to their human-generated, expert content. If they stop providing such access, training future AI models—particularly in emerging fields or topics—will become difficult and lead to even more errors and omissions. So it is in Google's best interest to highlight the sources of its AI-generated content.

Instead of being in Google's knowledge graph, an SEO should aim to be the brand used in the AI-generated content. Having subject matter expertise will be more important than before to ensure that your content is seen as valuable. With only one reference slot for AI-generated answers, brands will need to compete for that coveted position as Google's AI answers continue to evolve.

## GOOGLE'S NEW AI MODE

AI Mode is a new feature introduced by Google that provides conversational chat-type capabilities within Google Search. The introduction of AI Mode is a major step by Google to respond to the threat posed by OpenAI and ChatGPT.

As of June 1, 2025, AI Mode became available to all users in the US (*https://oreil.ly/PARME*). You can expect this to expand to other parts of the world throughout 2025.

Figure 8-2 shows us how Google has integrated this into the search user interface. As you can see, the current UI has this as the first option in the menu bar, and this provides us with an indication of the priority that Google is placing on this feature.

*Figure 8-2. How AI Mode appears in the Google Search UI*

What is AI Mode? Put simply, it's designed to respond to user prompts with conversational responses. Like Gemini and ChatGPT, user prompts can be complex and include multiple parts and it can remember the context of prior user prompts, as well as other information about the users. It can accept text, voice, and images as input.

The authors expect that Google may make AI Mode the standard mode for certain classes of queries. For example, if the user query is informational and uses natural language to ask the question, it may be a candidate for a default AI Mode response by Google.

The impact of AI Mode will likely be significant. Some classes of queries will no longer receive the traditional Google Search experience. This will further lower clicks to websites, particularly for informational queries.

However, this doesn't mean that your opportunities for revenue will go away. As the role of AI in search continues to evolve, remember that the number of prospective customers for your products or services don't change as a result.

To deal with the challenges raised by these changes, you'll need to invest time, money, and effort to stay ahead of the curve and beat your competition in figuring out how to adapt. While this may seem like a burden, bear in mind that it's also an opportunity.

## UNDERSTANDING GENERATIVE ENGINE OPTIMIZATION

Google's AI-generated answers are becoming more commonplace, especially with search queries containing at least eight words. It's estimated (*https://oreil.ly/BTyn7*) that 25% of queries containing at least eight words have AI-generated answers. The SEO landscape has changed, and one prominent difference is that ranking in the top three results on Google isn't as big a win as it used to be. Now, you should begin to target GEO, aiming to include your organization's web page as a reference in Google's AI-generated results.

Figure 8-3 displays results for the query "What is a STEM degree?" Notice that the left is Google's AI answer and the links on the right are the references. GEO targets the reference links on the right of the AI-generated answers to a query. Also notice that the "Show more" button expands more information, and no other links are displayed above the scroll. This means that being the first result in the traditional search results (which comes after the AI-generated answer) is not as effective as it used to be.

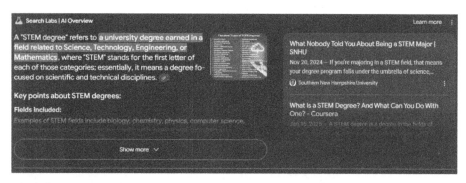

*Figure 8-3. AI-generated results for the query "What is a STEM degree?"*

GEO targeting gives organizations more visibility. As Google increases the percentage of search results that include AIOs, you will need to focus more on being one of the reference links in the AIOs. You can see in Figure 8-3 that only two reference links display in the AIO. GEO will be much more competitive than traditional SEO, where being on the first page would bring in good click-through results, especially for the first three results above the fold.

SEO practitioners should know that GEO results could change their metrics. Being in the top three search results could bring in the same traffic as being in eighth, ninth, or tenth place prior to the advent of AIOs. Even if you succeed in becoming one of the references in Google's generative AI answers, remember that users receive an answer to their question without even clicking through to a third-party website. When this answer fully addresses the user's question, they won't need to click through to any of the source websites for more information. However, even if users don't click as much as they do on traditional search results, there is still brand value in being present in the AIOs.

In Figure 8-3, we get an answer to our search question, but some users might ask a follow-up question about receiving a STEM degree, so being a reference follow-up link in the AIO might result in some traffic to your website. For example, a user might ask "where" or "how" to get a STEM degree. As an SEO practitioner, you might bring traffic from these queries. Ideally, your organization would be in the reference links where potential students could get more information about STEM degrees.

To be more competitive with GEO, you'll need to take a slightly different approach to content optimization than you have with SEO, which includes:

*Authoritative citations*
> Using links to authoritative resources is a common SEO strategy, but working with academic journals, government resources, or large, trusted news publications will boost your credibility and potential GEO visibility.

*Statistics and useful data*
> Many queries return numerical data to the search users. Adding your own authoritative information in the form of statistics, data from your studies and research, or numerical information that answers a query increases your authoritative signals.

*Direct answers to the query*
> AIOs rely on ingested information from pages that answer questions or can formulate an answer to a question. Make sure your content directly answers the question a user asks a search engine. You can obtain questions from third-party tools like Semrush or Ahrefs.

*Authoritative content*
> In addition to answering the question directly, your content must also address closely related background and questions that users are likely to be interested in.

Success from GEO strategies also differs from traditional SEO metrics. Instead of focusing on clicks and visitors, GEO focuses on impressions based on your organization being included in SGE results. Generally, SEO content focuses on being authoritative and digestible by a broad audience, but GEO content must be much more specific at targeting a search query. Keywords can still be integrated into GEO-targeted content, but they must be embedded into contextual answers to search queries with statistical information and authoritative citations to back up your research.

### Note

In GEO, we don't think about ranking for keywords, but instead we think about how comprehensive we are in covering the topic and subtopics related to user needs. Nonetheless, keyword research can still provide us insight into what areas are of interest to users.

Some elements of SEO can carry over to GEO. For example, media elements are still relevant, but they should be highly authoritative. Infographics that AI crawlers can ingest and interpret can be easy for users to read quickly and better understand the topic, but they can also be used in AIO content. Designing your content to address user intent is still important. If your content is weak in addressing this intent, that will decrease user satisfaction with your site and harm both your SEO and GEO efforts. GEO will search for relevant content that answers the user's query and filter out irrelevant, spammy, or poor-quality content.

Protecting your organization from content theft is an issue you need to consider. Most important is determining if you want all your content to be crawled. It's common for SEO practitioners to work with a domain's *robots.txt* file to block certain bots from crawling and indexing parts of site content. For example, you might have a low-quality page that you want to block from being indexed for quality-signal purposes. The same will be true for GEO crawlers. You might need to block some AI bots, but you should enable them from the major generative AI tools covered in this book, as you do want visibility on those platforms.

### Note

Not every bot will honor *robots.txt*, so SEO practitioners should monitor visitor statistics for malicious AI crawlers in addition to monitoring for malicious bots.

## THE INFLUENCE OF QUERY INTENT

Google is a business like any other, so it can be expected to change its methodologies based on the expectations and desires of its users. If users are happy with AI-generated results, then SEO professionals should expect Google to work with AI to create snippets at the top answering customer queries.

Using AI-generated answers isn't always beneficial, though. Again, it depends on the nature of the query. As an example, suppose a user asks Google to display the "best vacuum cleaner." The "best" vacuum cleaner is subjective, and AI is not valuable for opinions (people generally want the opinions of experts or other people who have used the product). Having a short snippet at the top of search results isn't beneficial for users in this scenario either because they likely want to see real human reviews and need to decide on purchasing the best appliance. Shopping and ecommerce SEO professionals will still find themselves working to rank their sites in these types of traditional search results as AIOs will have less of a presence. That said, Google is likely going to value human-generated content for these types of queries, such as Reddit, review sites (*Trustpilot.com*, *ConsumerAffairs.com*, and others), or other forums, and SEO practitioners will have to address those types of sites ranking higher—and potentially AI summarizing those results in the future.

The way Google handles search experience will depend on searcher intent, whether it's to make a purchase or to find information. Evergreen content will likely find itself below AIOs or other search snippets generated by AI at the top of the Google results. SEO practitioners can still try to get their own sites linked within these snippets, but it will be much more competitive, with the possibility of only one to three sources listed in them. In addition, traditional search results will be pushed below the fold and have less value than they do today.

Instead of manual execution of a search query, AI could be used to predict what searchers want on their smartphones. For example, suppose you always look for presents for your child on your smartphone. Generative AI could ingest common search queries you use and predict that you need to buy a present year to year. It could even give suggestions before you perform a query. Google would need to adapt to include its service in this type of situation, where its search shows a list of items you could buy for your child's birthday. In this scenario, an SEO practitioner would want to ensure that their store is in the list of possible options for users to view and buy.

## THE IMPACT OF GENERATIVE AI ON BUSINESS MODELS

There are other ways the SEO industry will change. Some of these changes could severely affect business models. For businesses that are negatively impacted by generative AI results, their owners and SEO staff must find new ways to attract users to their products and services.

Some changes have already affected popular brands around the web. One example is Chegg, one of the best-known educational content providers. Chegg provides answers to quiz and test questions for students. In 2021, it had a database of 46 million answers to various student questions and a $12 billion market cap (*https://oreil.ly/QVp5l*). Students could send in questions and hope that Chegg's database had answers to these questions. Since the introduction of ChatGPT, students are instead turning to ChatGPT to get answers to their questions. ChatGPT provides answers based on a vast array of much of the world's information, while Chegg has answers to only 46 million questions, a small percentage of the world's information. Semrush data (*https://oreil.ly/_hOdA*) suggests that Chegg has lost more than one-third of its organic search traffic, and the company's market cap lost more than 80% of its value between February 2024 and February 2025.

Another example of how generative AI affects site business is any dictionary site. As you may know, users go to dictionary sites for answers to word definitions, synonyms, and antonyms. For a while now, Google has displayed the definition of a word directly on the SERP. Users no longer need to go to any dictionary site to find answers, but the definitions displayed by generative AI come from these dictionary sites. Getting your organization's pages into Google's generative AI answers will be critical for SEO professionals but very challenging, with numerous competitors vying for the same positions. Should you get your brand into the generative AI results, your page will be referenced. Users then can click the reference link to see more information directly on your site.

While generative AI search will undoubtedly introduce a shift in how we drive traffic to our sites, it is unlikely to completely replace search engines or our current SEO strategies. That said, we must adopt a hybrid approach that uses traditional ranking and optimization techniques alongside AI-driven techniques.

## Introduction of ChatGPT Search

In October 2024, OpenAI released its own search engine called ChatGPT Search. The search engine is still in its infancy, but it could become good competition for current search engines, mainly Google with its dominant market share. It appears that OpenAI is trying to break into the search engine market initially using a Chrome extension, and ChatGPT Search can also be integrated into Microsoft Teams.

Right now, if users want to find a product, they first need to know the product or attributes of the product. Users can ask Google questions, but they need to get close to understanding what they are searching for. One difficult aspect of SEO is covering content and sales for any search query possible that can create visibility in search for potential customers. The OpenAI search eliminates the need to cover search queries. Instead, SEO professionals need to find ways to get their products shown in ChatGPT Search.

Let's say your client sells cars. An SEO practitioner must create a content strategy to cover as many search queries as possible that users might use when searching for a product or service like what your organization offers. For example, some potential customers could be looking for eco-friendly cars, another group of people might be searching for cars that are best for long-distance commutes, and others might be looking for sports cars. The current goal of SEO is to show up in Google search results for various search queries. Ideally, SEO practitioners strive to appear in the first three results, or at least on the first page. Not every search query has the same search volume and intent, but SEO aims to drive traffic to your employer's site to then sell its product.

With the OpenAI search, people can now ask questions about the type of car they're interested in, and the LLM provides a list of suggestions. Google's search results are vastly different. Right now, Google doesn't give you a list of links to cars. Instead, it gives you links to discussions where people talk about cars. Let's look at the query "I'm looking for a car that's good for California driving and off-road trails" for both Google and OpenAI. First, let's look at the initial links in Google's search results, shown in Figure 8-4.

In Figure 8-4, you can see that some of the results are based on discussions or reviews provided by third-party sites. The results don't provide direct suggestions for car manufacturers or models, so users must click links and read more to figure out the best car for what they want.

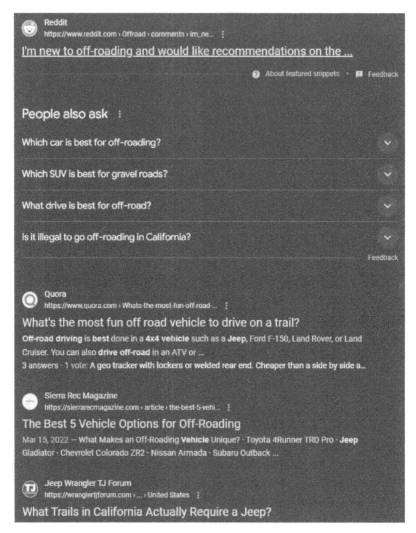

*Figure 8-4. Google's search results for "I'm looking for a car that's good for California driving and off-road trails"*

In contrast, OpenAI search gives direct suggestions for car manufacturers and models, as shown in Figure 8-5.

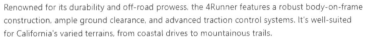

I'm looking for a car that's good for California driving and offroad trails

When selecting a vehicle suitable for both California's highways and its diverse off-road trails, it's essential to consider models that offer a balance of on-road comfort and off-road capability. Here are some top recommendations:

**2024 Toyota 4Runner**
Renowned for its durability and off-road prowess, the 4Runner features a robust body-on-frame construction, ample ground clearance, and advanced traction control systems. It's well-suited for California's varied terrains, from coastal drives to mountainous trails.

**2024 Jeep Wrangler Rubicon**
A classic choice for off-road enthusiasts, the Wrangler Rubicon comes equipped with front and rear locking differentials, a disconnecting sway bar, and impressive approach and departure angles, making it adept at tackling challenging trails.

**2024 Ford Bronco**
Revived with modern features, the Bronco offers various trims tailored for off-roading, including advanced 4x4 systems, terrain management modes, and a rugged design that handles both city streets and backcountry paths with ease.    ↓

*Figure 8-5. ChatGPT Search results for "I'm looking for a car that's good for California driving and off-road trails"*

As you can see in Figure 8-5, OpenAI provides three direct suggestions. For an SEO practitioner, your new goal will be to get your organization into these search results. You may even need to create content that can be used in generative AI search results for better conversions once users land on your pages. You may want to shift toward focusing on earning placements in generative AI search results.

## Progression of Generative AI Technology

In December 2023, DeepSeek was released to the public. The new Chinese models are open source—meaning the parameters for models are made publicly available (also known as *open weight*)—and DeepSeek is seen as a significant competitor to OpenAI. A major feature of DeepSeek that attracts users is its user price (*https://oreil.ly/pGggM*). Users pay about $3 for one million tokens, which give you about 80,000 words. Compare this cost to $15 on OpenAI for the same number of tokens. This inexpensive alternative to OpenAI could mean more users flocking to DeepSeek instead of using OpenAI. Cheaper generative AI could attract more users to content creation and other SEO benefits at a much greater scale at a lower cost. The lower cost also gives smaller businesses the opportunity to leverage generative AI.

DeepSeek is a lower-cost LLM option, so it's likely that others will find ways to reduce the costs of training these models. Cheaper costs benefit SEO practitioners who might not work for an organization with high-end marketing budgets, which brings more competition to the industry. You should expect to see many other new LLMs emerge over time. These will give SEO practitioners more options and add competition to the market. Even with other LLMs in the market, SEO will not be eliminated. Some of the work will now focus on GEO and become more competitive for brands.

## Conclusion: Preparing for the Future of Generative AI and SEO

Although generative AI is rapidly advancing, it falls short of consistently producing complete and accurate humanlike output. Images, videos, and text often have elements that give them away as being created by a bot. Although sometimes the signs are subtle, as people become more familiar with AI-generated content, their ability to discern it will grow.

Nevertheless, generative AI will continue to evolve, and we can expect significant improvements in its ability to create more humanlike output. It might take many years to get there, but generative AI is still at the beginning stages of its evolution. While it might seem like generative AI cannot replace human-made art or writing, it will improve. In years to come, it will be less and less distinguishable from human-made content. Automation using generative AI will make SEO tasks more efficient, and some jobs traditionally done by humans might go away. SEO practitioners will need to "skill up" and find ways to work with new search engine strategies: strategies that include focusing more on the AI snippets at the top and less on displaying links to users.

DeepSeek and other innovative generative AI technology have already reduced the number of "hallucinations" when models don't have the right answers. Instead of relying on human researchers, generative AI can work with thousands of academic journals and sources to produce more accurate answers. The benefits will continue to grow, and generative AI will become an important asset for critical industries like health care. For example, doctors could get information about treatments based on symptoms to help them better treat their patients. It's likely that many other industries will leverage generative AI to speed up productivity and provide a better quality of life.

Improvements to generative AI are already in process, but raising the quality of AI output will take time. It may not happen next year or the year after, but it will within a few years and over the next decade. The generative AI you know today will be vastly different and more accurate in 10 years. For SEO practitioners to keep pace with generative AI, they need to continually experiment with changes, adapt their strategies, and work with AI models that produce output for their brand. If you aren't using or planning to use the advanced technologies discussed in Chapter 6, then you risk being left behind.

Staying at the forefront of SEO in the age of AI requires experimentation. When you find an SEO strategy that works, continue to refine it. As AI technology advances, your SEO strategies must keep pace to ensure continued relevance and success for your organization.

# Index

## Symbols

# About the Authors

**Eric Enge** is currently the president and cofounder of Pilot Holding, Inc., a digital marketing agency that assists organizations with their SEO and AEO/GEO needs. He was previously the founder and CEO of Stone Temple Consulting, a leading SEO agency, which he sold to Perficient in 2018. Eric is also coauthor of *The Art of SEO*, which had its fourth edition released in September 2023. He is a regular speaker at major industry conferences, including Search Marketing Expo, Pubcon, and others. Through these conferences and his books, Eric strives to help attendees and readers learn how to get far better results from their digital marketing efforts.

Eric was also named 2016 US Search Personality of the Year by the US Search Awards, 2016 Landys Search Marketer of the Year, and 2018 Search Personality of the Year by the Drum Search Awards. In addition, Stone Temple Consulting won multiple awards from these organizations. You can follow Eric on X (Twitter) at @stonetemple.

**Adrián Ridner** is cofounder and CEO of Study.com, a leading online education platform serving millions of learners worldwide. With deep expertise in product-led marketing and AI-driven growth, Adrián has consistently demonstrated how strategic use of generative AI can increase revenue, enhance efficiency, and deliver industry-leading profitability at scale. Under his leadership, Study.com has received multiple recognitions for innovation, including being named one of Fast Company's Most Innovative Companies and earning Adrián Silicon Valley's 40 Under 40 award.

Adrián doesn't just speak about AI and digital marketing—he actively applies these strategies, building and scaling successful ventures while continuously evaluating what drives real results. Recognizing owned media as the most powerful channel to effectively engage large audiences and build meaningful relationships with customers, Adrián has pioneered methods that leverage generative AI to transform content creation, improve organic reach, and drive substantial revenue growth. He puts these innovative approaches into practice every day at Study.com and within the companies he advises, providing real-world validation of what works—and insight into what doesn't.

With a background deeply rooted in technology, Adrián has built his career at the intersection of software engineering and digital marketing. Before launching Study.com, he founded and scaled several technology-focused companies, employing SEO-driven strategies to effectively reach massive audiences and drive revenue growth. Adrián also serves as an advisor to various technology companies, sharing insights on leveraging generative AI to enhance growth and reshape product and marketing strategies.

# Colophon

The cover illustration is by Susan Thompson. The series design is by Edie Freedman, Ellie Volckhausen, and Karen Montgomery. The cover fonts are Gilroy Semibold and Guardian Sans. The text fonts are Minion Pro and Scala Pro; the heading and sidebar font is Benton Sans.

# O'REILLY®

# Learn from experts.
# Become one yourself.

60,000+ titles | Live events with experts
Role-based courses | Interactive learning
Certification preparation

 **Try the O'Reilly learning platform
free for 10 days.**